The Great Triumph

A Memoir of Courage & Devotion

JEANNE ESTELLE SADDLER

THE GREAT TRIUMPH
A Memoir of Courage and Devotion

Jeanne Estelle Saddler

Amara Press
Washington, DC

Published by Amara Press

Cover Design: mypublishedbook.com
Cover Images: Courtesy of the Author
Interior Design by: mypublishedbook.com

ISBN: 979-8-218-78961-9

Printed in the United States of America.

Contents

For my amazing mother, Thelma Jean Richardson (1920 – 2019),
whose love and strength were her legacies given
to our family and all who knew her.

"And so our mothers and grandmothers have,
more often than not anonymously,
handed on the creative spark,
the seed of the flower they themselves never
hoped to see – or like a sealed letter
they could not plainly read."

–Alice Walker

Introduction

Despite humble beginnings as a sharecropper's
daughter in the segregated South,
she never seemed poor.
Although she attended college later in life,
she was always among the most cultured
and well-read individuals in any room.
Gathering her strength and goals from her parents,
her faith, and the early mentorship
of a prestigious Black couple,
Thelma Jean Richardson made her life a great triumph,
infused with deep love.

Chapter 1:

Toot

Toot, just six years old, and Otis, a long-legged nine-year-old, trudged along the red dirt road leading to the dilapidated school-house for colored children in McCormick County, South Carolina. The cool morning air carried the bright songs of cardinals and sparrows. Rabbits and field mice scurried a few feet from their path, unwilling to give up the country road to creatures that didn't threaten their daily routine. A soft breeze surrounded them with the sweet smell of dogwood trees in bloom.

Idle daydreams and thoughts of new games to play at recess filled their heads even though sharp stones often cut through the thin soles of their shoes. On that day, the young cousins were glad to escape the chores that fell to them in a family of sharecroppers. Otis' job kept him scurrying around all day to fetch water for the workers to drink when they could take a brief break from picking cotton. Toot had to sit under a weeping willow tree and care for her older sisters' babies, fanning flies away from them and then carrying the wailing infants to their mothers who would nurse them in the middle of cotton fields.

It was 1926 on the rural western side of the state. It was an era when young Black children, like generations of their ancestors before them, had to learn quickly who they must be and how they must behave outside their small homes. Young white children, whether they were poor or the offspring of rich planters and loggers, were also learning quickly that their tan and pink skin made them special.

Otis warned his younger charge to move to the side of the road because a big yellow school bus was approaching just yards behind them.

"Niggahs, niggahs, niggahs!" came the chant from the bus.

The white kids sang out their hateful message, some for their own entertainment, others to distract them from their own growling bellies.

Toot gathered all her strength as the lumbering bus covered her long, thick braids and neatly pressed school dress with dirt.

"I'd rather be a niggah than po' white trash!" she screamed.

Otis, afraid he'd be blamed somehow for his troublesome cousin's insult, stooped down and rolled into a ditch, hoping his reflection wouldn't be caught in the bus driver's side mirror.

"Ain't nevah walkin' with her again," he muttered.

No one knew why the eighth of nine children of a mulatto sharecropper, Red John Osborne and his wife, Josephine, had become such a spitfire. Born Thelma Jean Cornelia and nicknamed Toot, she proved capable and confident – sometimes dangerously so – even when she seemed too young to understand how the dynamics of hate, or even family life, could threaten her. It seemed her personality took hold before she learned that she was a poor little Black girl in a dangerous corner of South Carolina in the mid-1920s. Toot had her mother's luminous brown eyes and sharp tongue. She inherited her daddy's graceful stride, strength of character, and fiery determination. The mélange of parental traits created a pretty little girl who was known for her constant energy, wit, and readiness to solve any problem with a sharp verbal arrow, even if it was sometimes misguided. Some of her antics were certainly creative and mischievous enough to merit a beating for an older child. Just a week earlier, in the cool shade of a weeping willow tree, Toot gleefully worked with a few of her older cousins to build a rickety plywood cart they planned to attach to an old goat to give them a ride.

When the work was done, the bigger boys and girls refused to let little Toot go along for the first ride. They loaded themselves onto the plywood wagon and hitched it to a billy goat too worn-out to protest, pushing their excited youngest worker away. So, an angry Toot gave the old goat a hard, deep bite on his ear, making him buck up and dump all the kids on the ground, completely covering them with red clay dirt.

"I'm gonna beat you to a pulp so you'll never come 'round here no more," one of the bigger girls shouted as she ran after Toot.

Anna Mae, a sympathetic older cousin who admired the little girl's spunk, saved Toot by jumping in front of her and fighting off the other girl. She knew that Toot would surely be on her side next time.

Most often, though, words were Toot's weapons of choice. She would grab a few of them, sure of their emotion if not their meaning, and fire her verbal arrows at her victims before they saw her in the room. When she heard her dad spit out a common slur for the sharecroppers' boss, she knew it was perfect for her bossy big sister. So as soon as twelve-year-old Novela ordered her to do more than her share of work in the family's cramped kitchen, she was ready.

"You just a cinnamon bitch," Toot shouted out. The term was delivered with the little girl's triumphant march to the front of the shack with her little arms and thick, long braids swinging.

"And by the way, Novela – you better call me Thelma now - Daddy says I'm so smart that one day you and the whole family's gonna call my name to get help!"

Thelma's confidence and spunk took hold like wildflowers growing in dry rocky fields with little nourishment. Like thousands of Black families, her parents were bound as sharecroppers, a system that several decades after the end of slavery, still made their hard labor benefit only white landowners. The soul-crushing work of picking cotton never created enough for better clothing or the proper schooling on which to build a future.

For many years, the family got by – sometimes laughing with each other, most times angry at their fate, and always determined to make their way toward a better life. Little Thelma, the second to the youngest child in the Osborne household, often was the bright spot of humor and hope. Thelma watched her parents work on plan after plan to someday escape their meager existence in McCormick County, South Carolina. She absorbed their determination and dedication to hard work in equal measure, layering it onto her own natural energy and love of language.

Thelma's family was among the tens of thousands of African American families who sought a better life by migrating to the North and West. They traded the terror and humiliation of the rural south for the hope of jobs with reliable salaries and real schools for their children. Facing misery daily, they had no idea of the struggles ahead of them. But amid hope and terror, Thelma Jean Osborne grew and carried seeds of strength, determination and intelligence even though she did not know she possessed them.

Author's note: *This is the way my mother, Thelma, began her journey through the rest of the twentieth century and into the twenty-first. Mom would often tell my brother and me of her early childhood years. The beautiful country environment was dulled by too much heat and humidity, and the rich red and black soil tied poor people, especially Blacks, to back-breaking labor. On Christmas morning, she said her only present might have been an apple or an orange in a Christmas stocking.*

In that era, Blacks had to endure not only poverty, but also the constant threat of terror and violence posed by whites working to maintain their political and economic advantages. There were few, if any, escape routes to a better life. There were far too many petty acts of disrespect that sparked rage in proud men like her father.

The stories my mother told us were exciting and funny and, in her telling, more sad than tragic. They led me to understand not only who she was, but who I could become and what I might achieve if I took her lessons to heart.

The Great Triumph is her story. It is also the story of my extended family, who through love and conflict, achieved a measure of success despite the barriers erected against them in the twentieth century. The incidents retold here, though true, have been re-imagined and enhanced to demonstrate their effect.

Chapter 2:

Red John and Josie

Thelma's dad, Red John Osborne, a tall, handsome, and imposing man, was born in Georgia and had made his own way since his mother, Emma, died when he was just nine years old. Emma was an orphan and household servant to a white family. John was born after a young white nephew of her employers forced himself on the teenage girl, raping her after cornering her in an outdoor shed. The frequent sexual abuse of Black girls and women was almost always ignored and accepted at that time. It was one of the many brutalities that survived as slavery ended, continuing the trauma Black families had experienced for centuries. Although John's father later acknowledged his son, he was of modest means and did nothing to help Emma or the baby.

After his mother's death from pneumonia, Red John survived by doing odd jobs for any white family that would employ him and by living from time to time with any Black family that would offer him temporary shelter and food.

He treasured his memories of his mother's soft, encouraging words to her young son, winding her love and great hopes for him like a shield around his heart. At the end of a day's work, he would close his eyes and wait for an evening breeze to cool his brow. Then he would imagine that he was again lying with his head across her lap as she rubbed his back and smoothed his wavy black hair. He could feel her love surrounding him. Like her, he became proud and self-sufficient, developing a strong arm and even stronger character because of the kindness and cruelty of the people he encountered around Augusta, Georgia. He learned to hate the advantage his light skin often brought him, even though he was in no position to turn down any advantage that came his way.

For many years, Red John was able to work as a young assistant to a group of Black men who took on whatever work they could find. They taught the boy how to work and escape trouble in the unforgiving days of the Jim Crow South. The kind men gave him a sense of family. He beat back his loneliness, learning to laugh and play checkers with them.

"Hey little brother – you study long, you study wrong," they'd tease.

"No way, I'm gonna study long, get fast and strong, and beat all y'all old guys one day!"

Red John would laugh and dance around the checkerboard to the men's delight.

He learned how to put in cash crops like cotton and how to catch a boll weevil infestation before it went too far. As he grew stronger, John learned how to split logs for builders. He helped plant and harvest beans and peas, sweet potatoes, and melons.

When John entered his late teenage years - tall, ruddy and muscular with thick, black hair, he was often the target of white men his age. Beating them at a job – or God-forbid, catching the secret glance of a white girl – were constant dangers. Lynchings were common in the post-Civil War era during Reconstruction in the South. But there were also the petty violent rebukes that Black men endured that arose from a white man's sense of entitlement. The greatest danger: Red John knew his worth and his strength and would never "take-low" to another man.

One day, after he beat out a few white guys for a job by rapidly splitting logs in a railroad yard – in front of managers who didn't mind hiring a light-skinned Black man – his life was on the line.

That evening two skinny white boys jumped him on the edge of a nearby wood, certain that together they would dispose of their competition.

"Hey boy – you stop now so we can talk 'bout that job. You best not take it, darkie!" they shouted.

The boys caught up with Red John before he realized the threat. Just one of them would have been no match for him. He was taller and more muscular than they were. But the attackers armed themselves with heavy branches and surprised their target with what they thought would be a short fight.

Red John sprinted far ahead of his attackers, climbed a huge pine tree, and waited for the two to pass below him.

"Hey now, crackers," he called out as he threw large stones in a different direction to confuse the boys.

When he jumped back on the ground, he caught one of them and slammed his head against the tree and gagged him by pushing a small branch full of sticky pine needles into his mouth. Then there was time to overcome the second boy.

With no time to breathe deeply or rest, he ran for several miles, careful to remain in wooded areas, a safe distance from town or farms where a running Black man could be stopped and accused of any local crime. He felt secure when the afternoon sun warmed his back and assured him that he was running eastward toward the Savannah River which bordered South Carolina. Later that evening, he found a quiet, shallow bend in the river where he crossed into the state of South Carolina. After finding a secluded spot, the exhausted young man slept, mercifully delaying thoughts of how to approach the rest of his life.

Red John expected that making connections and building a life in a new state would be another hard and lonely hurdle. But then, a glimpse of beauty beckoned him.

The lovely vision was what seemed at first to be a soft blanket dangling from a room on the second floor of an open-air cabin. Josephine Martin, the beautiful young girl whose leg was the vision, quickly covered herself when she noticed the handsome man staring at her from a lush green field. As Red John worked on the property near her home in McCormick County, SC in the coming weeks and months, she made sure to catch his eye and build his hopes again and again.

Josephine - Josie as she was known to her family - had more schooling than most Black girls in the waning days of the nine-teenth century and could read and write well. Her family owned a small piece of property in an area that had already been divided up for sharecropping.

For several years, Josie and a few other of the Martin family's offspring had been allowed to go to school and play with the white landowner's children. The arrangement ended when the larger property was sold, and the new white owners wanted to get hold of any land owned by Black people. Josephine had heard if any woman in the family wanted to keep a piece of the land, they'd need a husband to help work it. More importantly, she already had her sights set on getting away from the South.

For years, Josie learned more than other Black children by hiding in a spot beneath the kitchen window of the big house and listening to white planters talk. "Y'all know the niggahs think they got the right to vote now," came the drawl of an old white planter. "Well, I'll tell ya how to handle them damn darkies. Just smile and tell 'em there's a nice little piece of meat or a little more sugar if they vote for your man. Then – all our problems is solved. We sho' ain't gon teach em' to read nothin."

And while the whites bragged to each other about their success at keeping her people down, they also often talked of a great world beyond their own rural existence. There were cities called Charleston and Savannah; there were big schools for white kids, more sweets to eat, dances and fun than she'd ever imagined. Josie wanted to one day see the world that was beyond cotton fields and dirt roads.

She dared to dream of a life away from everything she had known, even though such dreams were unheard of. With so much stacked against her family and all Black folks, Josie wondered if the handsome Red John Osborne would become the strong man to help her make something out of almost nothing and carry her away to a happy life.

Aware of her own good looks, she'd taken in the hungry stares and compliments men always sent her way. When she saw Red John, she decided to enhance her natural beauty with the laughter and flirtatious smiles of a girl who had been taught to keep such charms carefully hidden. To her surprise, she suddenly felt the rising heat of her own young womanhood, and brightened her large, jewel-like eyes with sweet smiles.

In her presence, Red John was reminded of his own playful early childhood and thought of his loving mother, the only real family he'd ever known. The sad memory was quickly swept away by Josie's delightful energy and her determination to overcome all obstacles in her way. For his part, John would lean on a hoe to come close to his sweetheart, hum softly and say,

"When you laugh, pretty girl, I hear that red bird sing."

Their courtship blossomed quickly. The grace of the universe descended on the handsome couple, although they had no assets between them save tender love and blind hope.

In the year 1900, John and Josie married on a breezy, warm October day. The scent of sweet magnolia trees surrounded them at the tiny New Light Christian Church attended by the Black tenant farmers around the town of McCormick. For Red John, the young girl with the untouched legs would become the family, the reason to smile, he needed so much.

Red John had become a trusted worker in the area, so Josie's family gave the couple a sturdy cabin and a small plot of land to work for a vegetable garden. The house had a living and dining area of medium size, a kitchen with a fireplace for heat and cooking and just one bedroom with a corn shuck mattress. Josie stitched curtains and bright gingham coverings for the table, chairs and dresser that John made. It was a decent start for the young couple. Each night, they shared their dreams of better days to come. For them, it was a beginning, but not nearly enough.

Red John was a fast and efficient worker – picking cotton as well as food crops – and he also hauled logs and collected turpentine to put extra money in a family savings pot. Josie had only to mind the family garden where she grew beans, tomatoes, and sweet potatoes for their own food. Because John had seen so many Black women work as hard as men in the fields, he insisted that Josie work only at home, and care for their children as they came.

Their money for food was limited and space in the small home soon became cramped as five children were born in their first ten years of marriage: Agnes, William, Floyd, Lucille and Mordel.

As the growth of the overall U.S. economy slowed in 1910, sharecroppers were making less than ever. Each year, almost all the proceeds from the sale of the cotton crop went to pay white landowners for fertilizer and equipment, with too little left to support the family. Because Josie's family owned their small piece of land, they were better off than most of the other tenants in the area, but still didn't make enough to create the life they hoped for.

"I'm workin' from 'can to can't' – from 'can see' in the morning 'til 'can't see' at night," he'd say, "an it all goin' to the big house."

He could only swear and curse the landowners at home, because "givin' jaw" to white men was the way to endanger his life or that of his young sons, Bill and Floyd, who watched his every move. He was determined to raise his sons to be proud men, even though the terror of the Klan's white-robed night riders could threaten at any time. John's rage at the insults that his people endured often would show; he remembered well the pain and struggle of growing up mostly alone, learning any trades he could from other Black workers to support himself. Now he worked as a sharecropper to maintain a tiny home and safety for his family. The circumstances he and most Black workers endured stabbed at his independent soul. When he saw other sharecroppers grin and shuffle or try to curry favor with white folks, he'd cringe and spit on the ground to signal his disgust to his sons.

"A man has gotta stand in this world – no matta what," he'd say.

Josie was secure with John's protection, but she still wanted more of the life she heard was somewhere beyond the sharecropper's existence.

"When we sit out on the porch, John, you always tell me to turn around or cover my legs when you see those old white men walking by. Fine, Sweetness and I thanks you and love you. But I surely got so much more inside this body and heart for you and our young ones . . . so many plans and so much sense that can't just go to keeping a garden and raising our babies. I got the same dreams any white woman has for her family. We got to go, John, and make somethin' of our lives."

Red John agreed, even as he thought of the horror he had seen on the back roads of Georgia and South Carolina. Grisly murders and constant degradations he wouldn't often discuss.

"You so right, my wife. Just biding' my time and savin' money," he answered.

To make things worse, their children were now old enough for school, but because the state gave little or no money to educate colored children, the little ones had to work in the cotton fields once they were old enough to stand and do small jobs.

Over the next ten years, John and Josie would have six more children, with four of them surviving beyond early infancy. Ezra, Novela, Thelma and Sonny all began life in the same forgotten corner of South Carolina.

Josie and the children attended New Light Christian Church where she had married John. Church was most interesting once a month when a minister from the African Methodist Episcopal Church visited New Light with his message of hard work and hope for a better day for her people. It was also a regular reminder of the slow pace of progress for her race and made her yearn for a way to escape.

In late April 1925, the lynching of an entire Black family in Aiken County, just about 100 miles south of Red John and Josie's home, changed everything.

On July 31, 2020, the Augusta Chronicle published a story detailing the kind of terrorist incident that was common in the American South for many decades. It was based on extensive research using newspaper accounts, books, NAACP records and U.S. Supreme Court opinions. A summary of the article is as follows: this lynching was like those that convinced the Osborne family to join the Great Migration and head North.)

While the Lowman family worked at various tasks around their home, the armed Aiken County sheriff and his deputies rushed onto their property accusing them of operating an illegal liquor den. In the struggle that followed, the sheriff was killed by stray bullets, after the white men killed the family's mother as she tried to shield one of her sons. The other family members – the father, two adult sons and an adult daughter - were arrested and charged with murdering the sheriff even though they weren't armed. After two days, the entire family was dragged from the county jail and lynched.

"We gotta get outta here and I mean soon," Josie erupted, her voice trembling as she shared the terrifying news of the recent lynching she'd heard about at church that Sunday.

Red John agreed in general but insisted on staying until he could save more money to feed the family and to find a way to move North. But now, Josie was sure there was no more time to waste. Fear contorted her usually peaceful face into a brown and red-tinged mask her children barely recognized.

For more than twenty years, Josie knew she had simply followed Red John's lead. He was smart, strong and cautious and had kept the family safe as she was tied to childcare. But Josie felt her own more aggressive nature taking over. She decided to push her husband as she'd never done before.

"You know those white men 'round here are scared of you, and they might make up any lie. We can't wait 'til they come for our boys! We can't wait 'til they snatch the girls..."

Thelma was just four years old. She would always remember the outburst she barely understood but would transform her world. She cried softly, while her older siblings sat all around her, frozen by fear and the angry truth their mother presented. Josie announced she would travel north to visit the one couple they knew in Detroit, Michigan and try to secure a temporary place for the family to live.

"No more wait & see, John! I'll go while you work for a little while. When I come back, we'll all have to leave or... As I said, this is life or death- mostly death 'round here," Josie said, retreating to her bedroom.

The pace of change for the Osbornes was not as fast as Josie hoped, but the lynching of an entire family so close to their home had sealed their fate. The attacks she knew occurred all over the South had reached their back door. Soon, the family's two eldest sons, Bill and Floyd, full of their mother's determination and their dad's strength, left South Carolina to look for work in

Washington, DC. The eldest daughters married in their teens to poor farm laborers who decided not to leave the area. Mordel, a smart but rebellious daughter, had left home to follow her brothers to Washington, DC.

By 1929, with more than half of the children out of their small home, Red John and Josie Osborne were finally ready to travel, to flee, really, the only life they'd known.

With the life they knew overcome by their desperate reach for safety in the unknown, the couple decided to use their last bit of strength to move North. After Josie's visit to the couple she knew in Detroit, Michigan, they decided to move to the city, reasoning that it sounded like a place made for people used to hard work. When most of the cotton crop was already harvested, Red John traveled to the city alone to look for work. After a few weeks, he was hired as a laborer by the Michigan Central Railroad. With that small stake in the North, Red John and Josie would move, taking their younger children, Ezra, 16, Novela, 14, Thelma, 8 and Sonny, 4, with them.

Grandfather – Red John

My Grandaddy was my protector, with his muscular, though aging, arms and his warm, comforting presence, full of the sweet smell of his pipe tobacco. His loving gaze was a beam of assurance as I walked the short half block to my house from the corner store, carefully balancing two double-dip ice cream cones he'd bought for my brother and me. He would often stay with us on summer days while both our parents were working, leaving for his house when they were on their way home.

But despite memories wrapped in love and gentle care, I can't recall ever seeing Grandaddy smile.

"Okay, baby," he'd say when I asked to comb his silky straight white hair. Or "You study long, you study wrong," he'd tell my older brother Darryl as he taught him to play checkers.

Most often, his face seemed full of memories and sorrows. He was overcome by anger once when he saw my brother tied to a tree in a game of cowboys and Indians. Such games were common in the 1950s when children were still taught, incorrectly, that 'Indians' were responsible for violence in the old West. Grandaddy had the look of a man who had seen hell and escaped without being consumed by it. And although he lived among us, he could never forget the sight enough to smile.

Even without a smile, I knew that with his gaze at my back I was safe – protected from all danger with every bit of bone, sinew and blood he could still claim.

Grandmother – Josie

It was clear to me that my mom felt neglected and ignored for most of her childhood by a mother who, she said, was just tired of the hard work of rearing children. Despite that criticism, I developed deep admiration for my grandmother, who died when I was just three years old. I was told she was a very attractive woman with a sharp sense of humor. She never got to enjoy much of the very comfortable middle-class life she knew existed, but she'd had the courage to push her husband and her family forward.

Because I was so often described as her favorite grandchild, I imagined that she was my guardian angel in heaven, looking out for me as I took my first uncertain steps in each 'new world' that I approached.

Chapter 3:
Detroit, Michigan - 1929

The family arrived in Detroit in October 1929, just as the Great Depression began.

To Black Southern country folks, the city – which had been built by and for the wealthy white industrial class – looked almost heavenly. Although the city thrived on its reputation as a hub for hard work and innovation, it was also evolving as a sophisticated center for business and culture.

In the late 1920s, gray stone castles of capitalism were built to create Detroit's own 'Wall Street.' The Penobscot Building, erected in 1928 and rising forty-seven stories was, at the time, the fifth tallest building in the world. The nearby Guardian Building was put in place the next year to house the Union Trust Bank and was noted for its colorful brickwork and Pewabic tiles, which were made of a copper-colored clay used and named by the local indigenous Ojibwa people. With a lobby that featured marble walls and floors, it was called a "cathedral of finance."

During the so-called "Roaring Twenties," Detroiters shopped at their own big department store, J.L. Hudson's. Local white families relaxed in the lovely grassy fields and playgrounds of Belle Isle, a 982-acre island park in the Detroit River which featured a 40-foot-tall marble fountain and its own casino.

By 1928, the city also boasted the Detroit Institute of Arts, an Italian Renaissance style structure of white marble, which became one of the premier art institutions in the country. The city's main library stood directly across the street, also built of white marble with mosaic-tiled ceilings. Detroit's public schools and libraries were second to none.

The Osborne family wouldn't see Detroit's great power landmarks until a few years after their arrival. First, they saw a city that contained clean, middle-class neighborhoods full of frame and brick homes built to easily withstand Michigan winters. Then they saw the area where most of their own people lived – called Black Bottom – a crowded, poor ghetto on the city's East side. The entire city stretched over nearly one hundred thirty-nine miles.

Although this northern "heaven" promised good schools for the children and an escape from the ever-present dangers of poverty and racial terror in the South, it concealed Detroit's own deep-seated prejudices and delivered new fears.

For the flood of Black immigrants from the South, Detroit in the 1920s, 30s and 40s was both dynamic and dangerous. The newcomers had heard there was a tough brand of racism in Northern cities, but the newly arriving Black Detroiters had no idea of what they would face or the tough, defiant people they'd become.

In the early 1900s, Henry Ford, Sr. and his engineers developed a method to efficiently mass-produce the so-called "horseless carriage," which had been invented in Europe, for a world still reliant on horse-drawn transportation. Ford's new assembly line helped build automobiles fast enough to make Detroit the center of the industrial revolution.

In 1914, Ford advertised that he'd pay unskilled workers five dollars per day in his Detroit factories. It was an offer heard not only on Southern plantations, but in hard-scrabble Appalachian coal mines, and in European fields full of hungry peasants.

The city's rough character was formed by the thousands of poor whites who were the first wave of workers attracted by the new auto industry and the supporting jobs that developed in smaller factories.

The early Black arrivals found only the most menial jobs open to them and were crowded into the Black Bottom ghetto on the East side. As the years went by, Ford Motor and the Kelsey Hayes Wheel Co. began to hire "colored" workers for their plants, along with the Michigan Central Railroad and the U.S. Post Office.

The newly arriving Blacks had to fight more than economic competition. For generations, American popular culture had used every available tool, including minstrel shows, movies, and advertising to defame Blacks as ignorant and sub-human. It was a deliberate campaign to incite racial hatred, reinforcing the belief that poor whites were inherently superior people while distracting them from their own struggles with ignorance and poverty.

White entertainers appeared in blackface in productions such as "The Pickaninny Band" and "All Coons Look Alike to Me." Packaging for everything from laundry soap to rice and pancakes featured caricatures with large pink lips and dark skin. Children's books weren't forgotten. There were titles including "All the Funny Little Darkies."

So as waves of Black newcomers arrived in Detroit at a rapid pace, whites steeped in this brand of racism used violence and intimidation to maintain their dominance over the city's jobs and good neighborhoods. On several occasions, hundreds of white workers walked off their factory jobs to protest the hiring or promotion of just a few Black men.

And in the 1920s, it was common for mobs to attack the homes of Black families that dared to move into the city's white neighborhoods. 1925 was an especially difficult year.

The Arc of Justice by Kevin Boyle explains the atmosphere the Osborne family encountered in their new hometown. The homes of two prominent Black doctors were attacked by mobs of enraged whites after the doctors moved their families into a white neighborhood. The attacks were led by the Ku Klux Klan, which was surging in popularity as it campaigned against not only Negroes, but Jews, Catholics and foreign-born white workers.

Dr. Alexander L. Turner, the respected chief of surgery at Dunbar Memorial, the city's small Black hospital who also had appointments at two of the city's white hospitals, was one of those attacked. He and his wife, Leota, were well-known pillars of the community.

Dr. Turner graduated from the University of Michigan's medical school and later received his surgical training at Freedmen's Hospital in Washington, DC, which later became Howard University Hospital. He began practicing medicine in Detroit in 1910 and became the first Black general surgeon in the city. Dr. Turner also founded two drug stores while still in medical school.

A tall, dark-skinned and stately man, Dr. Turner was accustomed to his leadership role among Black doctors. He was humiliated in 1925 by a white mob that broke into the home he and his wife had occupied just hours earlier.

Fearing for their lives, the couple fled the home, crouched on the floor of their chauffeur-driven car, until they reached Dr. Turner's office, where they were forced to hand over the deed to their property to the Tireman Ave. Improvement Association, an arm of the Klan. Though the couple remained in the city for many years after the incident, the horror of the scene never left them.

During another 1925 attack — on the home of Dr. Ossian Sweet – one of the white attackers was killed after Dr. Sweet's brother fired shots into the air above a mob that gathered to pummel their stately bungalow with rocks and hard coal. With police detectives, neighbors, media and politicians working and campaigning against them, all 11

Blacks in the home that night were charged with first degree murder.
As news of the case spread across the country, the NAACP made it the
primary example of the extreme housing discrimination that blacks faced
in many cities.

The association raised enough to hire the renowned trial lawyer
Clarence Darrow, who secured a not-guilty verdict with his impassioned
oratory, supported by the legal strategy of another distinguished liti-
gator, Arthur Garfield Hayes. The Sweet case became a national scandal
and was the major case used to raise funds to establish the NAACP's
Legal Defense Fund.

When the Osborne family arrived in 1929, Detroit's hostility
toward the "colored race" as Blacks were called then, was set in
stone. The railroad job Red John was promised had disappeared,
most likely given to a white man in need as the Depression began.
To keep food on the table, Red John did odd jobs for rich families
and also worked with the federal government's Workers Progress
Administration (known as the WPA), which provided work for
impoverished men during the economic collapse. Often, he was
assigned to sweep snow off shallow ponds near the Detroit River so
wealthy white children could ice skate.

The Osbornes spent most of that first hard year in Detroit
living with Mabel and Eddie Willis, their friends from South
Carolina, an older couple with no children at home and a room to
rent. There, they absorbed Detroit's recent history by listening to
Sister & Brother Willis.

After Red John returned from doing any odd job he could
find, the adults would order the children to bed before talking about
any frightening incidents and listening to WJR -AM, the city's main
radio news station.

"What happened to Dr. Turner and Dr. Sweet ain't been
forgotten," Brother Willis warned. "We call it 'up-South' here. Yeah,
the jobs and schools are better, but the mobs still attack our folks

when they see us getting' ahead. Keep all the kids close if you can."
The radio news programs backed up his warning each night. As
the Great Depression took hold and some factory jobs disappeared,
angry whites mounted turf fights to maintain their advantage over
Blacks, Jews or any unwanted immigrants. Red John and Josie now
wondered if they'd made the right move in coming North, but at the
wrong time.

Red John leaned back and inhaled deeply as he smoked his
pipe, hoping the heavy smoke would somehow strengthen him.

"Hard work, protecting my family – that's all I know, Bro
Willis. I'll have to make it work," he murmured as he packed fresh
tobacco into his pipe and lit it.

He pushed the bittersweet smoke into his lungs rapidly,
steeling himself with each inhalation. Once again, he would be a
determined warrior facing unfair odds.

Thelma, now eight years old, listened carefully to absorb
the adult talk, sitting unnoticed by a cracked door. The aroma of
leftovers from their dinner of beans and ham hocks mixed with the
sharp scent of whiskey and smokey sweet pipe tobacco. Cold air
seeped through cracks in doors and windows as she began to grasp
the rules of her new world.

When Red John finally found work at the Kelsey Hayes
Wheel Co., the family rented a small house on Bangor Street, just
on the edge of the old West side where Blacks were beginning to
integrate several blocks.

The Bangor Street homes were often in need of a new roof or
siding to keep out the cold but were better than the apartments to
be found in the city's old Black Bottom ghetto.

The home had a small living room, a separate dining room,
two bedrooms, one bathroom and a medium-sized kitchen. It was
the size of an apartment, but had a small yard shaded by an apricot
tree – a curious advantage in a city like Detroit. A basement coal

furnace provided ample heat in the winter – unless money was short, and the family had to burn as little of the fuel as possible until they could afford the next delivery.

Thelma and Novela shared the bedroom across from their parents' room, and Ezra and Sonny slept on a mattress on the dining room floor. Sister and Brother Willis had given them a few pieces of furniture and helped them get donations of other items from folks who had saved enough to get better furniture for themselves.

Thelma would lean on the old pine dresser that sat next to a small window in her room and daydream about what this strange, cold city would mean for her and her family.

The acrid aroma of soot from industrial furnaces wafted over the neighborhood, and the loud clanging of machines pressing steel was common. Detroit winters set-in hard by mid-November. Beautiful, gentle snowfalls often were followed by ice storms that bit through the thin second-hand winter coats and boots the Osbornes had acquired. By the end of the year, streets that had looked serene under moonlight and dim streetlights became depressing corridors of steel gray slush.

Faced with hard winters and the need to always look for extra work each evening because his job at the plant paid so little, Red John was bone-tired most days. When he returned to their home during brutal Detroit winters, he would slump to the floor near a cast iron radiator in the kitchen, pulling off his thin wet gloves and knit cap. Thelma would run to sit by his side, warming his big hands, blistered from shoveling snow, in her own soft hands.

"That's my baby," he would say weakly, "my little piece of gold." His love and encouragement were the highlights of her evenings at home.

Detroit's high schools proved too difficult for Thelma's older siblings. Ezra and Novela rarely attended school and dropped out when they realized they were many years behind their classmates because they'd received so little schooling in the South. After less than two years in the city, Ezra left home to join his older brothers who then worked as cab drivers in Washington, DC.

Novela – a tall girl with a fine figure who had inherited Red John's light skin – concentrated on her ability to attract boys. Josie tried her best to save Novela, recalling her own flirtatious girlhood. But the pretty country-girl mother didn't know how to keep her daughter away from big city temptations.

Novela would stay out with boys who would drop her off at home late at night without bothering to escort her to the door. Some of the neighbors began to refer to her as "that big Yella' gal" who had "run out."

Thelma, on the other hand, was still a child – anxious to please and able to latch on to new opportunities. When Thelma first entered her new school, Sill Elementary, just a few blocks from her home, she was amazed at the school's attractive brick exterior and the shiny wooden desks that gleamed from heavy furniture polish.

The building was a stark contrast to the broken-down school she'd known in the South that offered Black children a poor education for a short time each year. Thrilled to have such a beautiful new school, Thelma became obsessed with completing all her work perfectly.

During the 1930s, the city's public schools were so effective they were considered a model for many other big city school systems. At Sill Elementary School and later at Condon Junior High School, Thelma began to absorb books and literature well beyond her grade level. She won spelling bees and essay contests, repeatedly surprising teachers when they realized a young colored girl had prevailed over so many white classmates. She also became the family's most dedicated member of the historic Tilden Street African Methodist Episcopal Church, singing in the children's choir and performing in holiday pageants.

Sadly, because she was deeply disappointed in Novela, Josie reacted by becoming strict and harsh with young Thelma. She never attended awards ceremonies at Thelma's schools to celebrate the girl's achievements but would often warn her not to "bring disgrace on the family" like her older sibling.

"Mother, was I just left on your doorstep or something?" Thelma said in tearful frustration one day. "Nothing I do seems to matter to you."

Josie slowly began to see that she was neglecting her most impressive child. She tried to become a better mother to Thelma, but her change of heart came too late to equal the great bond between Thelma and her dad.

When Josie began suffering from rheumatism and a serious heart condition, the stately Dr. Alexander Turner made a house call to treat her. As Dr. Turner packed his medical bag to leave the Osborne home, the skinny ten-year-old Thelma meekly approached him and asked for a job. The doctor had noticed her two older siblings sitting idly by, disinterested in their mother's condition, so he was impressed by the child's moxie. Dr. Turner told her she could come to his home after school each day to wash the dinner dishes and dust the furniture for his wife. She would earn seventy-five cents each week.

Thelma's first job marked the beginning of the most impactful years of her childhood. Her parents didn't object, as it was common in those days for children to perform household chores in wealthier homes. The Turner home was just six blocks away from the Osborne household.

The Turners were childless. When Dr. Turner met the Osborne family, and the charming young Thelma approached him for a job, he thought the girl might be the solution to the sadness he and his wife had felt since the home invasion. Thelma went to their home every day after school for many months, and eventually, with her parents' permission, stayed with the couple full-time.

The arrangement continued for four years, and the Turners treated Thelma like a daughter. Dr. Turner would let her ride with him as he made house calls, instructing her to hide on the floor of his fancy Pierce Arrow sedan until he returned.

Mrs. Leota Turner, however, had the most profound and lasting influence on Thelma. With the help of her uncle, Frederick Loudin, who had performed with the renowned Fisk Jubilee Singers of the historically Black Fisk University, a young Leota Henson had studied piano for two years at the Conservatory of Music in Leipzig, Germany. When her uncle started his own choir, Frederick Loudin's Jubilee Singers, Leota became the group's piano accompanist and traveled with them for six years, performing in England, Ireland, Egypt, Australia, New Zealand, India, China, and Japan.

When Leota Turner welcomed Thelma, a charming, smart, and inquisitive child into her home, she took great pleasure in introducing her young charge to much of what she'd learned through her travels and her formal education.

The grand, sophisticated lady with glowing brown hair would now discuss, without condescension, the World War I history documented in the painting on her living room wall, "The Sinking of the Lusitania." Thelma gained a basic overview of the world, its continents, countries and various peoples. She was dazzled to hear Mrs. Turner refer to the grand sweep of human history from ancient philosophers to the Middle Ages and eventually the founding of the United States. The lessons were exciting and enhanced her confidence.

Thelma was especially thrilled to learn about the great opera star and actor Paul Robeson and the writers and artists of the Harlem Renaissance. For the first time, Thelma learned that her people were creating impressive literature and beautiful music and art.

Thelma was Mrs. Turner's shadow and visited the city's most impressive new locations including the Detroit Institute of Arts, the main public library building, and the beautiful Fox Theater which featured red marble columns, Persian and Indian architecture, and massive crystal chandeliers.

Black history was always part of her lessons. Mrs. Turner explained that the Second Baptist Church, located downtown, was founded by former slaves in 1836 and later became an important "station" or hiding place on the Underground Railroad. Thelma was also a proud little helper to Mrs. Turner who founded the Colored YWCA and served as its first board chair.

When the Turners vacationed at their summer home in nearby Mt. Clemons, Michigan, Thelma went with them, enjoying boat rides on the Clinton River and learning to play croquet, a European sport popular in elite American society at the time. The town was one of the few in the Midwest where prosperous Blacks could vacation. It featured a health spa, the Mt. Clemons Hotel and Mineral Baths.

During those summers, no longer was she a poor girl from the rural South, but a beloved young 'daughter' dressed in pretty resort wear, skipping along at her 'parents' side. Thelma's voice often rang out full of carefree play with newfound friends. "Hey Lisette, hey Gracie! I'll race you on the beach back down to my folk's house. Ready set, go – you can't catch me now!"

Her life with the Turners was everything she had longed for, a world of culture, refinement, and possibility. It became the model for the future she would work tirelessly to build for herself. She loved the couple's elegant French Provincial furniture, and absorbed everything Mrs. Turner taught her, including the rules of etiquette and how to set their dining table properly with gold-edged fine china and real silverware. Thelma saw that with a great education; she could become a grand lady like Mrs. Turner.

Leota also proved her mothering abilities by comforting Thelma when her monthly period began, gladly instructing the now girl-woman how to rinse her stained bedding in ice cold water.

The Turner home offered more than a beautiful contrast to her family's poor surroundings. At home, Thelma was baffled by the contrast of knowing that to her dad, she was the family's precious gem, and yet feeling she was an afterthought to her mother.

The Turner's love and attention was, for Thelma, a long summer shower on a parched garden. Thelma beamed with happiness when Mrs. Turner would say:

"You're my shining star, little girl. You have the sharp mind, the carriage, and looks of a fine young lady."

The couple's education and class were beacons for Thelma, proof that her natural intelligence and self-confidence could create a great life someday.

The life of luxury was cut short when Red John told Josie they might lose their brightest, most successful child, and insisted that Thelma return home. The Turners begged the Osbornes to allow them to adopt Thelma, promising to give her a first-class education. Although the request was denied, the years with the Turners had turned a confident and precocious young girl into a determined, savvy young lady. Nothing would ever be the same.

The Influence of the Harlem Renaissance

My mother once said her chest would fill with pride as she thought of a short Langston Hughes poem that had become a favorite when she lived with the Turners.

"My People"

"The night is beautiful,
So, the faces of my people.
The stars are beautiful,

So, the eyes of my people.
Beautiful, also, is the sun.
Beautiful, also, are the souls of my people."

Chapter 4:

A Deeper Sense of Home

Thelma returned home a girl transformed – one who had glimpsed a different, exciting world. She now carried brand-new hopes and dreams but had little idea of how to make them real. Most of all, she knew she wanted to continue to excel in school and then perhaps attend college at Howard University in Washington, DC. She dreamed it might be possible, especially with two older brothers already living in the nation's capital.

Founded in 1867, Howard University had become a mecca for African American students and intellectuals. From its earliest days into the 21st century, Howard became the premier institution where Blacks could attain a first-class education and go on to lead lives as respected leaders in Black communities around the country.

It was the home-base of the Black philosopher Alain Locke, known as the Dean of the Harlem Renaissance, who encouraged Black writers and artists to look to their own history and to Africa as sources of inspiration for their work.

The university's professional schools were also critically important – with the medical school's establishment of Freedman's Hospital and the historic role of Howard's School of Law.

Charles Hamilton Houston, the dean of the law school from 1929 - 1935, devised the attack on the segregationist theory of "separate but equal" that had ruled the lives of Black Americans since the collapse of Reconstruction in the 19th century. Houston was often called "The Man Who Killed Jim Crow."

His brightest student, and later his colleague at the NAACP's Legal Defense Fund, Thurgood Marshall, won the landmark 1954 Supreme Court Decision in Brown v. Board of Education of Topeka that sounded the death knell of legal segregation.

Young Thelma had just begun to understand that there was such a place where her people were the great thinkers and where determined lawyers were preparing to fight for the rights of the Negro race. She only knew she hoped to be a student at Howard and just maybe work toward those same goals.

When Josie arrived at the Turner's house to say that her daughter must now return home, Thelma was very much the embarrassed teenager. Her mother looked like the country woman she was, heavy-set now, after suffering from a heart condition for the last couple of years and wearing a faded blue gingham cotton house dress and anklet socks.

Josie quickly surveyed the Turner's pink and white tufted French Provincial furniture and European paintings on the walls. Then there was the elegant Mrs. Turner, who wore silk stockings and a lace-edged lavender dress with a starched white collar. The scene reminded Josie of the homes and the life she had heard of as a girl when she secretly listened to rich Southern planters talk.

Josie had never been one to envy another woman's life or possessions – until now. But she quickly realized it was beneath her to let those feelings show. True class - the kind not related to wealth - had always mattered to her. Like generations of women of color before her, she summoned the proud, worthy lady deep in her own soul.

As she held her head high, ready to thank the younger woman and simply leave with her own child, her heart softened as her eyes met Mrs. Turner's. She recognized in those eyes a kind of longing and sadness she had known when she lost two of her children as infants. Josie understood that pain but could not bear it again herself. There was no way to control the outcome even though the two women realized what the day's decision would mean for the young girl they both loved.

Josie took Thelma's hand as she quietly thanked the Turners for their loving care of her daughter. With her good fortune clear, she left holding on to her now prized possession. Thelma followed her mother home in silence, tears dampening her cheeks.

Thelma walked through the door of her parents' home to stay after four years when she had only visited every couple of weeks. Red John greeted her by wrapping his long, strong arms around his daughter and swinging her around the living room with delight, singing,

"My baby's back! My baby's back!"

Her little brother Sonny, now 9 years-old, skipped around his dad and sister, joining in the celebration.

Josie continued through the small living and dining area to the kitchen to start dinner. She glanced to her left and saw the bathroom door was cracked and knew that Novela was listening as John and Sonny welcomed Thelma back home. Josie knew a storm was coming. She'd watched over the years as her two youngest daughters traded sharp insults. Novela, in her early childhood years, had been the family's pampered light-skinned princess, with chubby cheeks and adorned with straight hair. ("I'm a little teapot, short and stout," she would sing and twirl around in front of any adult who noticed her.) But after Thelma became a toddler, she was the one who caught everyone's attention. Instead of looking for compliments, Thelma would try to start a funny conversation.

("Hi – Did you come over to help my daddy kick a cracker's behind or just to eat my mamma's cake?" she once inquired.)

Thelma was feisty, loving and pretty – all at once.

Josie saw the jealous rage rise in Novela whenever her sister was the center of attention but assumed it would disappear as Novela grew up. Instead, sibling envy became a strange and permanent part of Novela's personality. Red John was the most captivated by his baby daughter and didn't seem concerned about Novela's growing and obvious jealousy. To him, Novela had been another sweet daughter that he would love and protect. But little Thelma had always been a daughter full of honey and vinegar; a lively child who engaged his mind and heart and seemed destined for great things. The tension between the sisters continued throughout their lives.

As the welcoming celebration ended, Red John told Thelma to go put her clothes away and went to the porch to smoke his pipe and talk to Brother Willis who had come to the door.

Before entering the bedroom, she would once again have to share with her sister, Thelma passed by Novela who was applying make-up in the bathroom, arranging her light brown curls to frame a face that could, like a light switch, flip between light and dark moods in an instant. She studied her reflection in the bathroom mirror with practiced confidence. There was only room for one person to stand in front of the sink in the cramped bathroom.

White tile with a thin green tile border covered the walls, almost to the ceiling. Novela had spread her make-up – red lipstick, powder, rouge and black mascara – on the closed toilet seat.

"Hey Black Gal – what you doin' back here?" Novela said, slyly mocking her sister with a name their older brothers had used for their brown-skinned sister, but in an endearing way. "Thought you was still scrubbin' floors for that ol' doctah and his uppity wife."

Thelma bristled. She hadn't done any heavy housework for the Turners – just dusted the furniture and washed dishes and had been treated like their daughter.

"Oh no, Big Yella Gal," Thelma quickly replied with her own brand of derision. "Just thought I'd take a break from cruisin' on the Turners' boat and eatin' fine dinners to come see how many boys you're spreading your legs for these days."

Novela felt the cut.

The girls' argument continued at dinner that first night Thelma was at home.

"Oh, we got a maid and a little bad cook in the house now," Novela said as Thelma helped their mother set the table and serve the evening meal. "Come on, Black Gal and serve me like you did Mrs. Turner."

"Why of course I will, my dear sister," Thelma replied as she pulled a chair out from the table and with a grand sweep of her hand, invited Novela to have a seat.

When Novela, still determined to play the nasty game she started, lowered her backside about an inch from the chair, Thelma pulled the seat away and smiled as her sister tumbled onto the floor.

"You lil' bitch, I'll tear your ass up," Novela cried out as she scrambled to her feet and ran to attack Thelma, both hands extended.

The fight was over as quickly as it began when Red John stepped between his daughters, facing Novela with a scowl.

"There'll be none of that, Novela. Any blow to her will have to come through me first," Red John said, surprised by the anger he was now directing at his own child.

"You been makin' your bed around town for a while now. Maybe it's time for you to find a man who wants to buy a cow who's been givin' out her milk for free."

With that Novela stormed out of the kitchen to her room, trying to hide her tears. Once again, Novela had been reminded that she wasn't worth much in her dad's eyes compared with Thelma. The family then ate in peace and mostly in silence. Later, Josie took her older daughter a plate to the bedroom.

In fact, Novela had alienated both Josie and Red John. One day, when Josie asked why Novela was going out with the boyfriend of a dear friend of hers, the daughter flippantly replied that the boy was a "much-right man."

"That means I've got just as much right to him as she does," Novela explained.

With that comment, Josie became even more determined to marry her off before she brought more disgrace to the family. She concluded that Novela lacked ambition and only wanted to use her looks to manipulate those around her.

Novela believed she wasn't a "loose woman" but was simply exploring her power over people – a trait she thought would help her control her life. No one ever bothered to tell her that she had a sharp, strategic mind. With a great education and some encouragement, Novela might have become a formidable businesswoman, successful at playing every angle.

So, the young woman had decided to trade on the power of light skin and straight hair that made her stand out in Black America. It was a superficial thing that her father had always disliked most.

When the Willis couple mentioned a handsome young widower with a baby who was a member of their church, Josie quickly joined and insisted that Novela attend with her. Greater Redemption Church was very different from the Tilden St. AME Church where the Osbornes were members. Greater Redemption was an easy sell to Novela because it was an exciting Pentecostal or "holy roller" congregation, complete with people speaking in tongues and a livelier gospel choir. With her mother's blessing, Thelma continued attending Tilden St. AME.

After a few weeks at the new church, Novela caught the eye of the young widower. Josie reminded her wayward daughter to behave and demonstrate the ladylike qualities she had instilled in all her daughters. The Osbornes were relieved when the smitten young man proposed. Novela and Eddie Abner married, and she moved into his home.

Thelma was delighted to see her sister leave. With just their two youngest children now in the home, John and Josie were more relaxed. They spent more time talking to Thelma and young Sonny.

Unfortunately, however, Sonny would often angrily rage through the house or throw rocks at the apricot tree in the backyard. Born with a twisted mouth and small for his age, Sonny was often ridiculed and tormented by his classmates in school. He found it hard to pay attention to his lessons and his teachers took no interest in him or his struggles. Thelma took it upon herself to always soothe his anger by playing with him and helping him with his schoolwork.

"Come on my little buddy; it's just the two of us at home now, let's get this done."

Their bond would last a lifetime, even though she wasn't able to make Sonny into the dedicated student she was.

While living with the Turners, Thelma completed sixth grade at Sill Elementary School and started attending Condon Junior High School. Condon, which was located just a few short blocks west of the Osborne's home on Bangor Street, had been built just fifteen years earlier as the first school intended to serve as a junior high school. It was an imposing brick structure and accommodated about six hundred pupils.

Thelma continued to excel at her schoolwork there and because of the lasting influence of Leota Turner, she also would take the Grand Boulevard streetcar to the city's old Lothrop Library to borrow books or magazines that featured Negro artists.

Red John was proud to see that his little girl loved to read and decided to draw her closer to him and get to know her growing hopes and dreams.

When Josie told him their daughter had become a young woman in another home, and that the Turners wanted to adopt her, he worried about her safety although he would never talk of such things. He also feared losing the child who had always been the brightest spot of love and laughter in his home.

Now in his early fifties, John knew he had done all he could to do right by his children, keeping them well-fed and safe, but something about all the work of rearing them had left an emptiness in him he couldn't name.

His oldest sons, Bill and Floyd, became strong, proud and capable men, and left South Carolina in their late teens to drive cabs in Washington, DC with a group of young Black men who had started their own cab company. They had hoped for a similar success. Ezra, a younger son, had joined them there. Red John's oldest daughters, Agnes and Lucille, had married in their mid-teens and started families as was the custom in the South at the time. Mordel, the smart but rebellious daughter, had left home early, followed her brothers to Washington, worked as a maid for a series of white families, and began drinking heavily. Bill, Floyd and Mordel eventually moved to Detroit after the success they hoped for never materialized in the nation's capital. The District of Columbia was still very much a Southern city.

But despite all Red John's years of sweat-soaked work in cotton fields and lumber yards, his constant efforts to shield his children from lynching and lechery, despite the freezing walks home from Detroit factories to save the six cents on a streetcar fare – his older children rarely turned to look at him; to see the man who had saved them. They were too busy walking their own hard roads. Now, during long evenings as he watched snow cover everything but his aching back and his weary, wandering mind, he decided to try to find in his paternity something more than hard labor.

"Come here, baby. Tell your old dad what you had over there at Dr. Turner's good enough to make you want to stay," Red John said, calling young Thelma to his side. "You know we missed you and we still love you so, so much. . ."

Those few words from her father began the long talks that would shape Thelma just as much as her time with the Turners.

She told her dad she had learned that Blacks in places like New York City had become great, important people - writers, artists and musicians. She told him about the Harlem Renaissance and a big movement with the idea that there is a "New Negro" who would no longer let white people keep him down. Thelma explained that those artists focused on regular, hard-working Blacks, not those who held themselves apart because of skin color or their own success. Getting more excited as she talked, Thelma brought out of her room a copy of a poem symbolizing the new movement that Mrs. Turner had given her and read it aloud to her dad.

"*If We Must Die," by Claude McKay,"* Thelma began.

Her voice trembled nervously as she wondered if her dad would like poetry. Red John, satisfied with having started the conversation, leaned forward in his old easy chair, packed his pipe and got ready to listen. Thelma could see her mother leaning against the kitchen entrance to their small dining room, listening, too.

> *"If we must die, let it not be like hogs*
> *Hunted and penned in an inglorious spot,*
> *While round us bark the mad and hungry dogs,*
> *Making their mock of our accursed lot.*

If we must die, O let us nobly die,
So that our precious blood may not be shed
In vain; then even the monsters we defy
Shall be constrained to honor us though dead!
O, kinsmen! We must meet the common foe!
Though far outnumbered let us show us brave,
And for their thousand blows deal one death-blow!
What though before us lies the open grave?
Like men we'll face the murderous, cowardly pack,
Pressed to the wall, dying, but fighting back!"

Sensing her parents' interest, Thelma read the poem's last line with a great flourish and then saw them erupt in applause and whoops of appreciation and laughter. Her dad was deeply moved.

As Josie served dinner, Red John told Thelma for the first time about his escape from the two crackers in Georgia who had set upon him in the woods after he beat them in a competition for a job splitting logs. The poem had reminded John of the constant danger of being lynched or beaten and maimed and left to die. It had taken all the cunning, smarts and strength he could muster to overcome the two men, knock them unconscious and then escape across the border to South Carolina. It was the fight that made Red John the courageous man he became. Now he saw in his baby daughter the same kind of courage and hunger to do well in life.

John did all he could to encourage Thelma's interests, and the girl blossomed. Thelma began to see how much her poems affected her father when she read the *Langston Hughes'* poem, *"Mother to Son."* She started gently . . .

"Well son, I'll tell you:
Life for me ain't been no crystal stair.
It's had tacks in it,

And splinters,
And boards torn up,
And places with no carpet on the floor –
Bare."

. . .but stopped reading half-way through as she saw a tear roll down her dad's cheek.

She realized the poem reminded him of his mother, who died when he was just nine years old.

During the family reading sessions – that often lasted late into the night – Thelma began to see her own parents in a different light. She learned of her father's strength and courage as he grew up on his own after his mother died. She saw and came to admire in him the same kind of character, race-pride and striving for a better life she saw in Dr. Turner. Her mom grew in her eyes as well. Although Josie never had the chance for the kind of education Leota Turner had, Thelma could see that she, too, greatly valued education and stressed that women always must uphold their personal honor and the honor of their families. She learned much more from Red John and Josie during those long evenings than her older siblings had learned.

She had long observed the proud bearing of both her parents and adopted it herself. But now she heard stories that had been passed down to her parents of long-ago slave rebellions.

They explained to her the courage and hard work of Southern Blacks who tried for years to get from under the share cropping system. Too often, Blacks were lynched, shot and burned to death for their pride, ambition and daring. "Root little pig, or you'll die a poor hog," her dad would say as he explained his many schemes to earn more money for the family.

Josie would often talk about the need for women to be financially independent, if possible, and willing to put men in their place when they tried to take their honor. She told the story of a slave woman who taught her daughter to ward off abuse that too often came the way of Black women from their masters, saying

"Fight. And if you can't fight, kick. And if you can't kick, bite!"

The racial terror of the old South, and then the new but familiar problems once they moved North, along with the Great Depression worked to ensure their lifelong dreams of a better, easier life remained just dreams. This evening with their ambitious young daughter renewed their hopes.

Thelma and Her Parents

My mother's great respect and tender care for her parents affected me deeply. Because I saw how she cared for my grandparents, I developed a deep understanding and gratitude for what was given to us by our elders, those who held our hands as little ones. Even though my brother and I witnessed bitter verbal arguments between our parents and clearly saw our dad's physical intimidation of our mom, she always insisted that we treat him with the utmost respect.

"Honor thy father and mother," she'd say, quoting the Bible, "that your days may be long upon the Earth."

Chapter 5:
Dreams Deferred

As the reading sessions continued, John asked his daughter to focus on the big news stories of the day. Many evenings, she came home with a newspaper borrowed from the Lothrop Branch library - The Detroit Free Press, The Detroit News, or the Black weekly-The Michigan Chronicle, which began publishing in 1936. The Chronicle was a great source of information on famous Black artists like Paul Robeson, whose great baritone was heard in opera halls around the world, as well as the beautiful Lena Horne, a young Black singer and actress who was beginning to make a name for herself in New York City.

Each evening, Thelma enjoyed reading the news to her dad, carefully placing the emphasis and energy where it belonged while her mother cooked dinner. John would settle into his chair after work with his pipe packed, ready to listen as he smoked.

"Where's my Precious Gem," John would call out happily. "Come on now and read to let old Dad know how the world is fallin' apart."

Thelma read the news about the early days of the United Auto Workers Union and how poor working men like her dad were standing up for their rights against the wealth and power of rich auto magnates like Henry Ford.

In the process, her appetite for current affairs, politics, and race relations grew steadily.

She and John followed the work of a young legal director for the United Auto Workers, Ernest Goodman, who later won the admiration of Black Detroiters for successfully taking on civil rights cases in the city and across the country. Thelma began to think she might one day find work in law or politics.

There was also encouraging news about the development of the new Social Security system, designed to help everyone suffering from the abject poverty of the Great Depression.

Everyone the Osbornes knew was poor, struggling just to get by. As the nightly reading sessions continued, Thelma became the family expert on the economy and the promise of help because of President Roosevelt's proposal for social insurance. In the early days, however, Social Security was little help to many Blacks who didn't work for large companies.

By the time Thelma entered high school, her academic skills were stronger than ever because of the nightly reading sessions and the focus on current events at home. The Detroit Public School system was in its heyday in the 1920s and 1930s and was so good it was considered a model for other big city systems. Young Thelma was ready for everything that was offered.

Thelma attended the city's large, well-regarded Northwestern High School located at the busy intersection of West Grand Boulevard and Grand River, about a fifteen-minute bus ride from her home. Although Black students weren't placed in the advanced-level college prep track, Thelma outperformed white classmates. She loved literature and read more of Shakespeare's plays and sonnets than any of her classmates. Her reading carried her to China. The books of Pearl Buck, including "The Good Earth", became favorites.

Because she knew of the war brewing in Europe from reading the newspapers to her dad, she learned everything she could about history and current events. The constant struggles of African Americans were of primary importance to her.

In September of 1936, Thelma, her Black classmates at Northwestern, and certainly Blacks across the country were all walking tall because of the young Black athlete Jesse Owens, who won four gold medals at the summer Olympic games in Berlin, Germany. Jesse was well-known in Detroit because in 1935 he'd already set three world records and tied another in less than an hour at a Big Ten Track meet in nearby Ann Arbor, Michigan, the location of the University of Michigan. That feat was known at the time as "the greatest 45 minutes in sports history." Then during the Olympic games' track & field events in early August of 1936, Owens used his sports prowess to show Adolph Hitler and the world that whites were *not* the master race. The precious moment was fleeting. When Owens returned to the U.S., no white athlete would race him, and he was forced to compete against racehorses to earn money.

Before that dismal backlash, Thelma found a way to celebrate Owens' victories – but one she certainly didn't expect. She was full of information about the Harlem Renaissance and proud of Jesse Owens' accomplishments. In a sudden moment of reflection, she decided her role on the practice squad for Northwestern's girls' swim team offered a way to celebrate the confidence growing inside of her. Someday, Black girls would be allowed to compete at official swim meets. But for now . . .

Whoosh! Swoop!!

Her dive into the frigid blue-green pool at Northwestern High School was perfect – landing Thelma just beneath the surface at her swim team's practice session and creating the exact combination of buoyancy and speed she would need to prevail over the arrogant team captain, Liz Smith.

Then her slender, long brown arms whipped into the crawl and her more muscular legs beat the water furiously, propelling her well ahead of her opponent. Lap and flip . . . lap and flip . . . lap and flip – the team's only Black member felt she was on fire as she showed off her aquatic skill. It was 1936, still the early days of integrated school sports in the city, and she wouldn't be allowed to compete against the city's other varsity teams in official swim meets.

"THEL - MA!! THEL – MA!! THEL – MA!!," came the muffled sound in the gym, piercing through the extra-tight swim cap she wore to protect her neatly pressed hair.

"THEL – MA!! THEL – MA!!" – and suddenly she realized her usually aloof white teammates were cheering her on to victory over Liz, a captain who was always quick to brag about her speed in the pool and her popularity with the boys who admired her long blond hair and perfect figure.

"YAAY - - THEL – MA!! YAAY!! YAAY!! YAAY!!" the chants continued. As Thelma completed her victory lap, she saw the team's coach, Miss Marsh, go back into the locker room to retrieve her coffee, as was her habit.

"You're still just a NIGGAH," Liz spat, humiliated and enraged as she ended her swim, a full half a length of the pool behind the less experienced teammate she rarely acknowledged in any way.

Suddenly, Thelma's joyful fire ignited a simmering rage. With all the strength she could muster, the 16-year-old grabbed the hateful Liz and pushed the red-faced girl underwater in the deep end of the pool, holding her there as Liz struggled. She released her hold when her still delighted teammates - who were at that moment standing at the edge of the pool - warned her that the coach was coming back into the pool area. But Thelma wasn't finished.

"Hey Liz – you know I got that speed from my Uncle Jesse Owens – you heard he won a gold medal at the Olympics, didn't you? Got anything else to say to me now? Swallow that water first,"

Thelma taunted as the vanquished captain gagged, holding onto the side of the pool.

The team left for the locker room, where the girls showered and dressed in uncomfortable silence. No one reported the incident, thereby saving Thelma from punishment and Liz from more embarrassment.

In that moment, Thelma remembered her six-year-old self, screaming insults back at the white kids in a yellow school bus as it covered her dress with dirt - when anger and determination first called forth her fighting spirit.

As her strong academic performance continued, Thelma knew it was time to call in the promise her two oldest brothers had made to let her live with them while she attended college. But as she neared graduation, Bill and Floyd ignored her letters pleading for a chance to stay with them in Washington, DC while she visited Howard University.

As the weeks wore on without a reply from her brothers, Thelma cried often, staring out the tiny window in the bedroom she'd first settled into as an eight-year-old. She felt closed-in and locked away now, only able to see the narrow walkway between her house and the small, dilapidated house next door. Through that narrow passage, she had watched all of Michigan's beautiful seasons that she'd come to love, pass year after year.

She picked up a copy of a *Langston Hughes* poem, *"Dreams,"* that she had copied from a book while living with the Turners. *"Hold fast to dreams,"* she read once again. *"For if dreams die, Life is a broken-winged bird that cannot fly."*

Thelma cried until she escaped into sleep.

By the end of the school year, with her graduation nearing, and Novela safely married off, Thelma noticed her mother had now started to imply that she should think of marriage as well. Thelma reminded her mother that she'd chased away a nice boy about a year earlier when Josie was still consumed by Novela's behavior. Josie laughed. "Little girl, I'm not worried about you attracting young men, and I know you'll make a good choice!"

Mom's Great Swimming Victory

My mom stunned both my brother and me with this story. It revealed that she possessed all the determination, courage and race pride she'd noted when discussing the dramatic actions of others. The mother we knew was friendly, even-tempered and so very intelligent when she addressed adults, and would happily engage babies and children of all races in the same loving, playful manner, showing them that the world is a wonderful place.

We also knew Mom always said "she'd fight a bear" to protect us. This story of her fighting spirit proved that her comment was more literal than comical.

Chapter 6:
Duke & Dutchess

During the summer before her senior year, a cousin introduced Thelma to a handsome, fun-loving young man from Alabama, nine years her senior. Reynolds "Duke" Saddler had so much beguiling charm that he made John and Josie agree to allow their daughter to go out with him. His manners and dress were impeccable. He told them of his very religious parents who were still in Alabama and his older siblings who were already established in the city.

Thelma was charmed as well and looked forward to the family dinners with Duke's sisters and brother and their families. A few times they went for Sunday drives in the countryside, holding hands in the back seat of his brother-in-law's car. Duke would gently tease her and insist that she give him a kiss each time they passed a red barn.

Her boyfriend's softer charms were almost always on display. He possessed a rich, golden-brown complexion much like Thelma's and a warm and welcoming smile that suggested, as the old folks would say, that "butter wouldn't melt in his mouth." He was of medium height with a muscular build and was a good dancer who could gracefully escort a girl around the dance floor. With his joking and teasing, he easily attracted attention at any gathering. On the surface, he was a happy-go-lucky country boy who could drink with the guys and be a magnet for the girls.

Family lore said Duke – who was called "Dude" in his hometown of Irondale, a hamlet just outside of Birmingham – had to leave home for Detroit in the dead of night after a Ku Klux Klan lynch mob targeted him for what was perceived as flirting with a white girl. They had even shown up at the Saddler home with rifles.

His parents, H.Y. Saddler and Estella Reynolds Saddler were well-respected members of the Black community in the area. H.Y.'s business making and selling charcoal gave the family a good income, compared with most Blacks in that time and place. Known but not openly discussed, was the fact that Estella's biological father was a white man. So, the couple and their five children never experienced sharecropping and lived a better life than most Black families in the area. They were very religious, stayed within the Black community, and their children frequently had white playmates.

Nonetheless, the children, especially the boys, knew there were lines they could never cross. As young adults, all the Saddler siblings left Irondale to make their way in Detroit. Geraldine, the eldest, left first with her husband, and was followed by Raleigh the oldest son, and then Brooksie, Duke and Leon. Like other migrants from the deep South, they would establish themselves in a rented home one at a time, and then offer a room and advice to the next sibling to arrive.

Although Duke possessed perhaps the most lively, playful manner of the Saddler family, he could also easily slip into his Sunday-go-to-meetin' clothes and display the careful, follow-the-rules, respectful demeanor he'd learned so well from his parents, H.Y. and Estella. Those were the manners and values that quickly won over Thelma's parents. He easily talked with Red John about working in rural Alabama – both in his parents' large garden and for his father's charcoal business. And he also knew how to smoothly compliment Josie's great cooking and homemaking skills. He let them get to know the Reynolds Saddler who was indeed serious and hard-working.

There was, however, a somewhat volatile side of Duke Saddler. To be sure, he carried the anger of every Black man who knew he was overlooked and under-valued in America. He worked in Detroit's huge Eastern Market handling produce and making deliveries. The market, with its long, dirt-packed aisles lined with wooden bins full of fresh vegetables and metal stalls containing fresh, raw meat, was a country fair and oasis in the middle of a big city. The environment was familiar to Duke, but he had been frustrated by his unsuccessful attempts to get the kind of job he knew he deserved – as a skilled mechanic in the city's auto plants. He'd learned auto mechanics by working on delivery trucks for his family's charcoal business and could tell his skills were far ahead of the white guys who were often hired before him once he arrived in Detroit.

But on top of that justified anger about a better job, Duke was aware of his own intelligence, savvy and charm. He wanted the success and recognition he felt he deserved despite the racial animus of the day. His temper, which sometimes emerged around his immediate family, would grow worse over the years.

Duke's older brother, Raleigh, and his two sisters, Geraldine and Brooksie, had settled in the city before he arrived. Thelma admired the family's success.

Raleigh had earned a diploma from Cass Technical High School, which at the time was the equivalent of a high school diploma plus a highly regarded technical certificate.

Unable to convert that degree into the kind of jobs his white classmates won, however, he secured a postal service job and began to climb the ranks there. When Thelma met the Saddlers, Raleigh and his wife, Ernestine, already had three little children. Like Thelma, Ernestine had spent most of her life in Detroit and was clearly smart and friendly. Geraldine, the eldest of the Saddler siblings, was a pretty, buxom woman with a soft, friendly and loving manner. Brooksie, just two years younger than Duke, had a more energetic and flirtatious manner to add to her very good looks.

Duke's sisters' husbands, Arthur McAdory and George Carson, found jobs with Ford Motor Co. and spent years of hard labor before they were able to move ahead in the ranks at their factories. Through it all, the family members supported each other financially and emotionally during the Great Depression.

Because of her sister Novela's behavior, Thelma hadn't been allowed to date, and before Duke Saddler arrived, her mother had discouraged an interested boy who sought to date her. This time, however, Duke's charm won over the Osbornes and stole Thelma's heart. Duke carried himself in a sophisticated way, and had goals for a better life, just as she did. For the first time in her young life, Thelma felt the warmth and excitement of having a handsome suitor.

For his part, Duke quickly noticed and admired Thelma's interest in school and getting ahead in life, which added an unusual allure to a girl that was so beautiful. Understanding that his girl-friend was still a teenager, Duke carefully planned their dates to build her confidence in him and ensure she was having fun. He would often pick her up after school. On weekends, he would plan picnics in a park or invite her to Sunday dinners with his family. Several times they would just go out for ice cream cones, and Duke would be sure to get her back home before dark and leave a small bunch of flowers for Josie.

Thelma knew she had to be very careful, because Duke was already in his mid-twenties and clearly had "experience" with quite a few young women. Still, she believed she was the only girlfriend he had invited to have dinner with his family. So, as her heart fluttered, she gave in to what she thought might be the feeling of 'falling in love" that she'd only read about.

As the relationship grew closer and Duke's constant pleas for sex were unsuccessful, her charming boyfriend promised the thing he knew Thelma wanted most: he promised to send her to college if she would marry him. Although Duke was reluctant to set aside his days as a carefree bachelor, he, too, had fallen in love with a girl he was proud to have by his side.

Even though the college promise was one they both might have known was unlikely to come true, they let their feelings overcome their fear. Thelma finally agreed to elope on April 30, 1938. She knew Red John and Josie couldn't afford a wedding, and she had also promised herself and her parents that she would receive her high school diploma in June before deciding on her next step. As a result, the marriage remained a secret until her graduation day. She had no idea that more than 30 years of heartache and pain, mixed with joy and achievement, awaited her.

The young couple planned an early drive to Toledo, Ohio, just an hour south of Detroit, where it was common for people to elope and marry in that day. They wouldn't reveal their plans to her parents or announce their marriage until after Thelma's high school graduation. Thelma was nervous, excited and happy during the drive to Ohio. She wore her best dress, a pale, flowered dress of silky material, an outfit she'd only worn to church on Easter that year and had borrowed lovely jewelry from a friend. She noticed that her boyfriend was strangely silent. He admitted that he, too, was nervous, yet happy, contemplating the big step they were about to take.

They reached the Lucas County courthouse on a cool, sunny afternoon. The brick building was covered with ivy and surrounded by large welcoming oak and elm trees. They were directed to the Office of the Justice of the Peace to sign papers for their marriage license. There was a 20-minute wait for the official who would conduct their ceremony in a small room decorated to look like a chapel. Those minutes seemed to be hours as Thelma felt herself swinging between feelings of happiness and loneliness, between exhilaration and fear.

During her high school years, Thelma had gained so much confidence and had come to feel like an adult. She knew what was going on in the world and could even help her mom and dad understand official social security documents.

She was one of the top students at Northwestern and her classmates thought she'd be going to college. "Yes, Sweetheart," Duke said when he promised to help her attend college. "We'll just have to work hard and save the money first. That day will come." Now, with that slim hope of a promise, she would promise her body and soul to a man she loved but had known for less than a year.

She seemed to awaken from her anxious thoughts only when she heard – "Miss Osborne, do you take this man, Reynolds Saddler, to be your lawfully wedded husband. "I do," she whispered, realizing that it was much too late to back out of her commitment.

Thelma's fear that she had made a bad decision was soon confirmed. They arrived at the small Blue Bird Motel where they'd agreed to stay for just a few hours before heading back to Detroit to keep their marriage secret. The young bride prepared herself in the bathroom – all perfume and powder and anticipation – and sat waiting as her new husband took his turn in the bathroom and washed up.

A man transformed emerged, however, one who seemed to have become an angry monster.

"Why did you make me wait so long?" he demanded.

Most likely, Duke had been suddenly overcome with his own fear and uncertainty and didn't want to look weak or less than virile to his new wife. Strangely enough, he then attacked and set upon her with such force and cruelty that she began to cry and scream. Hearing the screams, the hotel manager ran to the room and banged on the door, demanding to know if there was an underage girl in the room.

"No man, this is my wife," Duke shouted back.

The manager left and returned in a few moments with a jar

of Vaseline. Thelma would later describe her first experience as a rape. However, Duke had never resorted to that kind of violence, and Thelma's innocence was so complete she didn't realize sex could be painful.

The newlyweds drove back to Detroit that evening through freezing rain – the kind of storm that was common in Southeastern Michigan until late spring. They rode in silence, Thelma in pain and shock at the horror of her wedding day, and Duke, now ashamed of his behavior.

He tried to convince his bride that she was just a tender girl and things would get better. Thelma wondered if she could get out of the marriage but realized her mom and dad wouldn't have money for a lawyer, just as there had been no money for a wedding. She suffered her injuries in silence for weeks, often trying not to pee because the urine burned the torn skin around her vagina.

Thelma's June graduation from Northwestern High School was bittersweet. She won several of the academic awards presented – best in the class in History, English and Current Affairs but she was missing the one thing she wanted most – admission to Howard University. She marched proudly in her cap and gown, nonetheless. She hugged her classmates and noted that most of the girls were announcing plans to marry. Many of the white boys had apprenticeships in auto shops and a few rich white boys would go to college. Only a very few Black students – those whose parents had sufficient money or connections – had college plans or apprenticeships.

But hearing the band play "Pomp & Circumstance" and seeing her own academic honors noted in the program, Thelma promised herself that this day would not be the end of her success in life. She held her head high and told friends she would marry first and go to college later.

That evening, Duke Saddler arrived at her home on Bangor Street with a large bouquet of spring flowers. He was invited to stay

The Great Triumph

for dinner to celebrate Thelma's graduation. He accepted nervously because he and Thelma had discussed announcing their marriage to her parents.

Before Josie served the special cake she'd made to mark her daughter's graduation, Duke began addressing the Osbornes in a formal manner. He declared his deep love for Thelma and said he hoped they would accept him as their son-in-law.

"I do apologize," he went on, "as we eloped and married in Toledo on April 30, without your blessing. But it seemed to me, given her high moral standards, and my desperate desire to have her by my side, it was the right thing to do."

Josie reacted with pure delight at the announcement, but Red John, having watched and silently understood his daughter's distress in recent weeks, simply gave Thelma a long, sad embrace.

"Never forget that Dad will always be right here for you," he said, holding up two fingers pressed together to symbolize their great bond. "You'll always be my little piece of gold, my precious gem."

The newlyweds' first home was just a rented room in the home of Duke's sister and brother-in-law, Brooksie and George Carson. For the most part, the Saddlers had always seemed to welcome Thelma with open arms. Brooksie was the exception to that rule. Although she was very pretty, she seemed to immediately see a rival in Thelma, who was younger and better educated. Brooksie had the same charming outgoing personality her brother Duke possessed and was accustomed to attracting all the male attention in a room. At family gatherings, she would make sure she was noticed as the best dancer, and she took it on herself to organize games and other entertainments. With a dark mole just to one side of her lip, her smile and eyes offered a "come-hither, fool, but just for a tease" sort of look. George, her second husband, was quiet and gentle compared to his wife, unless he was playing cards or drinking with a group of men.

The couple had two sons.

Thelma, on the other hand, was a beautiful girl still in her teens, so innocence added to her allure. She was tall with thick hair and gorgeous eyes. She was often compared to the movie star Dorothy Dandridge. Her perfect figure would quickly turn every male head in a room, especially when it was on display at dressy occasions. And because, unlike the Saddler siblings, she had graduated from high school in a respected Northern school system and was very well-read, her easy command of proper English and knowledge of current events was always noticed.

When Duke announced their marriage, Thelma's new brothers-in-law quickly decided on an appropriate nickname for the lovely new member of the family – "Dutchess" – a name that would be used for decades by everyone on the Saddler side of the family.

Brooksie began her attacks on her sister-in-law in petty ways. Claiming that she wanted to save on the gas bill, she'd tell Thelma she could only use the oven to bake at certain times – primarily after Brooksie herself had used it. Because the two women worked different hours, Thelma would often use the oven on her own schedule because Duke enjoyed having fresh cornbread every day. But she soon discovered why Brooksie always seemed to know, despite her denials, that she'd broken the silly rule because Brooksie would hide breadcrumbs in the back of the oven, which soon would become toast and reveal the transgression.

The most serious conflict began when Brooksie would accuse her husband George of always "looking at Dutchess." In the summer, Brooksie tried to joke, saying that George would wear dark sunglasses to hide his wandering gaze at his sister-in-law.

The last straw came when Brooksie turned her 'joke' into a full-force attack on Thelma.

After leaving the city with her brothers, Duke and Raleigh, to visit their parents in Alabama for a few days, Brooksie returned full of suspicion that something was going on between Thelma and her husband George.

"You're just prancin' around here thinkin' you're so cute and so smart," Brooksie shouted in a rage.

"Don't you know I see what you're up to? Tryin' to pull every man you see away from his wife," Brooksie shouted at Thelma in the kitchen, stunning both her husband and her brother who were playing cards on the front porch.

The men quickly tried to calm the attack, but Thelma, tired of putting up with her crazy sister-in-law, shot back on her own.

"No way would I ever do anything so low," Thelma said. "Everything I have is just for my own husband. But let me tell you, Brooksie, and don't you forget it – yes, I'm cute and very smart – you're just jealous because for years, I was up here going to school when all you could do was pick blackberries down in Alabama."

An awkward silence followed that exchange, and Duke and his young wife rushed to their bedroom and decided to move as soon as they could.

"How could you mess up our situation here?" Duke said as he struggled to keep his anger at his new wife from exploding into a loud argument. "We're living under their roof, you gotta show some respect."

They had been saving all their money for more than a year and planning to get their own place. Yet with one well-placed barb, Thelma had shown her in-laws and her husband the kind of fight she had in her. She'd often thought to herself, "I'll just bide my time, be good to my husband, and find a way to get away from this crazy woman."

Fortunately, Thelma already had been using her smarts, determination, and skill at problem-solving to find a new home. Her plan was to borrow as much money as possible from her dad, who had always managed to save more money than anyone she knew and combine that with their own savings. She also talked to old friends from Northwestern High School who had recently bought a house. Through them, she found one of the few Blacks in town who worked for a real estate agency and could help couples get a home. The agent agreed to loan Duke and Thelma half of the down-payment needed to buy an old two-family flat. Then they would rent one of the flats and use the proceeds to pay him back monthly until the debt was paid off with interest. The arrangement was relatively rare and was kept secret. It was a variation of the land-contract arrangement that often led to Black families losing their money and their homes in the mid-1900s. By pulling together extra money for the down payment and buying in a Black neighborhood, they were able to cement a deal.

Within a few months of the confrontation with Brooksie, Duke and Thelma were able to tell their shocked relatives that they were buying a two-family flat on Hazlett, just across the street from their family landlords.

The large white wood-frame home featured three small bedrooms, along with a living room, dining room, kitchen and bathroom in each flat or apartment. There was a separate furnace room for each flat in the basement and a shared backyard and garage. Duke and Duchess decided to live in the upstairs flat where they enjoyed the privacy of a large top porch that stretched across the front of the entire home. Because of their two salaries, the young couple soon furnished the home with an art deco style bedroom set, a mahogany dining room table and china cabinet, and a living room sofa with a lovely green and gold floral design.

Thelma's key role in the successful purchase of a home as well as the way she had put her sister-in-law in her place marked the beginning of a new and difficult relationship with some of her in-laws and with Duke. She and Brooksie would distrust each other for the rest of their lives. But she won the respect and great friendship of Duke's older brother Raleigh and his wife Ernestine. Geraldine, Duke's oldest sister, remained friendly and fair, but suspicious of Thelma's strong-willed determination to go her own way.

For his part, Duke could see that he had a partner that few other men had. Thelma had always found good jobs since they married and constantly looked for new ways to earn and save money. After the purchase of a home, she put aside the idea of going to college so they could easily afford to furnish it. She had won a job operating a freight elevator at the city's largest department store – J.L. Hudson's – at a time when most Black women were only hired as maids. She had taken a course in cosmetology and worked for a time as a hairdresser, and later at the Post Office. An excellent typist, she eventually won an office job in the typing pool at a downtown ad agency, Nelson & Associates. Duke was also doing well, even though he hadn't yet landed the job he wanted as an auto mechanic.

Thelma's only failure was that she had not yet produced a child. Soon it became clear that Duke still had an eye for other women but more importantly, his temper sometimes would rage out of proportion during an argument, bringing on nervous twitches of his hands and face.

In the early years of their marriage, his flares of temper might have been triggered by his annoyance at the attention Thelma would always attract from men or his anger at her quick verbal punches. Duke's nervous outbursts were sometimes difficult for him to control.

Once, when they attended a formal ball given by Detroit's Prince Hall Masons – a Black men's fraternal organization that Duke and his brother had joined – Thelma was dressed in a gorgeous lavender chiffon gown with a matching shawl and crystal earrings. The ball was held at Detroit's Gotham Hotel, a venue decked out with murals and crystal chandeliers which had been purchased to serve the famous Black musicians, athletes and entertainers when they came through the city.

During the ball, the Masons' top official, the Grand Master, noticed Thelma and with a deep honorific bow, asked her to dance. The band struck up a waltz as other guests cleared the floor for the group's top official. Halfway through the dance, however, an enraged Duke marched onto the dance floor and grabbed his wife's arm.

"I'm ready to go home," he growled. "I said, I'm ready to go," he repeated as the Grand Master asked for permission to finish the dance.

Thelma was pulled quickly to the hotel's winding staircase and shoved rudely down the stairs to the lobby as the other guests tried to regain their composure. Once they were home, Duke poured himself several shots of Johnny Walker Red whiskey and soon began to drink and angrily accuse his wife of flirting.

Thelma found herself reeling and crying in despair from his rough treatment. She wondered how her life had taken such an awful turn when she'd done nothing wrong. The public humiliation hurt as much as Duke's accusation. She wondered if she would ever find peace and happiness.

On another occasion, Duke prevented her from taking an apprenticeship she was offered through a cousin who owned the Stinson funeral home. She would begin by simply driving the car that held the funeral's flowers but would eventually be trained in every aspect of the lucrative business.

"Oh no. I wouldn't want her to cook my food if she worked with dead bodies," Duke told her potential employer. The offer was withdrawn when it was clear Thelma would be forced to choose between the apprenticeship and her marriage. Thelma often felt trapped and defeated as her efforts to get ahead were quashed but she never gave up.

"My Dad always said to keep on moving; root little pig or you'll die a poor hog," she thought to herself.

There were more personal disappointments as well. When Thelma heard that Duke was seen with other women and was probably unfaithful, she would cry at first and then turn her sharp tongue on him.

"You know, Duke, God sits high and looks low – in your case very low. You're just knee-high to a grasshopper," Thelma would shout.

She also had the ability to deliver insults that cut deep and often left Duke speechless. "You know my brothers said that maybe Duke is lookin' for a short woman. They said he's so short he should sue the city of Detroit for building the sidewalk so close to his asshole."

Unfortunately, Thelma was never able to connect the devastating impact of her verbal assaults with her husband's temper or behavior.

Although the couple frequently was the topic of neighborhood gossip, they stayed together. Duke would always try to make up and pledge to do better after their fights, and it seemed he didn't himself understand why his temper would rage. For her part, Thelma didn't want to endure the disgrace of a divorce, especially after having no children. So the couple made up again and again.

The beginning of World War II changed the couple's focus just as it changed the nation. Detroit was the first city in the nation to see a dramatic lift to its economy after the 1941 attack on Pearl Harbor led to an official declaration of war. Detroit's car factories were ordered to begin producing tanks instead of cars, hiring immediately shot up, and the city was nicknamed "The Arsenal of Democracy."

The city's new role greatly increased migration from the southern states. During the early 1940s about 300,000 white migrants and 50,000 more Blacks flooded into Detroit. Duke had become a good mechanic while working in Alabama with his father, H.Y. Saddler, who owned two trucks for his charcoal business. He tried again and again to win a job as a skilled mechanic in Detroit's factories. The newly arrived southern whites were, of course, quickly hired into the best factory jobs and became part of the city's expanded police force. The whites were alarmed to see that many Blacks were living well in Detroit and pushed for even more separation of races and discrimination.

In June of 1943, fighting between Blacks and whites broke out on Belle Isle, the lush park full of picnic areas and playgrounds on an island in the middle of the Detroit River. The battle grew in scale and spread across the Belle Isle Bridge and throughout the entire city. According to news reports at the time, the conflict was initiated by a group of white sailors who were angry to see Blacks allowed to use the park. It also was fueled by false rumors that a white woman had been raped and that there had been a retaliatory attack on a Black woman and her child.

The 1943 riot was one of the worst in the nation at the time. Federal troops were called in to end the disturbance, which lasted for thirty hours and left twenty-five Blacks and nine whites dead.

With World War II expanding to the Pacific, Duke was drafted later that summer and soon left for training at Fort Belvoir outside of Washington, DC. He would join a unit for more training at Fort Hood near Waco, Texas. Thelma was able to visit him at both bases before he was shipped overseas. Like thousands of other couples, the husband and wife were bereft and full of fear at the idea of being separated. She would always treasure a large, distinctive black cameo necklace he bought her while stationed in Texas before going to war.

Assigned to the U.S. campaign in the South Pacific, Duke fought on the islands of Saipan and Iwo Jima, serving in a "colored" unit that saw some of the toughest battles. Trained as a tank mechanic, building on skills he already had, Duke and his unit were assigned to sneak behind enemy lines and bring Japanese tanks and trucks that had stalled over to the American side. The battle for Saipan was later called the "D-Day of the Pacific."

Duke's memories of his worst battle during the war confirmed that idea.

Ping, ping – whap – bullets were bouncing off a small Japanese tank our team had repaired enough to drive slowly down a dark, muddy island road. When there was no gunfire, the sloshing mud just off the road was a greater concern - was the noise a crocodile or more likely the enemy, desperate to recover their own tank? Death was near us, just like trying to escape the Ku Klux Klan in the muddy backwoods of Alabama and Mississippi. Fightin' for my life and for a country that has never cared about my life. Gotta make a way. . .

Like all Black soldiers, Duke hoped his bravery and patriotism would one day mean equality and freedom at home.

He was on guard in a foxhole with his unit when, to his great relief, he saw the U.S. Marines raise the American flag on Iwo Jima.

Thelma missed him terribly and wrote every day. She lost weight because she ate very little, thinking of her husband eating only cold Army rations in a foxhole. As always, she followed every bit of news about the war in Europe and the South Pacific.

When the war ended and Duke returned home, he had the nervous symptoms of what was then called "battle fatigue." However, Duke was able to get a good entry-level job with benefits as a civilian missile mechanic at the local Army base, Fort Wayne.

Thelma began to follow a doctor's suggestion in a new effort to get pregnant. She was told to eat more and take a couple of health potions.

And because the war was over and they were comfortably settled in a home, she made another suggestion she thought would satisfy her husband. Thelma had learned early in their marriage that Duke had a son in Alabama who was born during a brief marriage before coming to Detroit. The marriage ended in divorce when it was clear it would be dangerous for Duke to return to Alabama permanently. Thelma met the boy and his mother when she and

Duke went south years later. Now she told Duke he should bring the child, now nearly fourteen, to Detroit so he could get a decent education. As usual, he had to agree that Thelma had a good idea.

With his mother's consent, Richard Nathaniel Saddler soon arrived in Detroit and started school. Rick and Thelma became good friends as she pushed him to achieve in high school and attend college. The teenager enlivened their home with his bright personality and harmless pranks. He enjoyed scaring his stepmother by sneaking up behind her as she prepared dinner and showing her a fat earthworm on a stick. Musically talented, Rick, who had played the trumpet since elementary school, eventually majored in music at Wayne State University in downtown Detroit.

With young Rick in the house, Thelma began to see that her husband's temper wasn't just a product of their relationship. Unaccustomed to parenthood, Duke would often explode in anger when his son didn't follow his rules. Despite those incidents, Rick was happy to have his father's attention after missing him for years and remained devoted to his family in Detroit and Alabama.

Despite Rick's arrival in their home, there was friction and discontent between Duke and Thelma. Family members and some friends began to whisper that Thelma was unable to bear children. Because Thelma had undergone an appendectomy when she was nineteen, those who knew of the operation claimed she had been "stripped" of her reproductive organs at the same time.

By the summer of 1947, Duke told Thelma that he wanted a divorce, saying that although she'd been a good wife, he had only gotten married again to have more children, and that hadn't happened for them. Ironically, she was able to announce to him at the same moment that her doctor had just confirmed her pregnancy.

Their son, Reynolds Darryl Saddler, was born the following April, and was called by his middle name.

Dad

In addition to having a volatile temper, my dad was responsible and serious, but he didn't seem to carry responsibilities lightly. I later concluded that his occasional drinking and even his jovial personality were used to quiet, if only for a time, his more serious, worried and angry side. His harrowing experiences before leaving Alabama, and later in the jungles of the South Pacific, probably also left him with a degree of a nervous condition that then was called "battle fatigue." After the Vietnam war, the same symptoms were diagnosed as "post-traumatic-stress disorder (PTSD)."

Even when things seemed stacked against him at work and he was denied promotions, he stuck with his position to support his family. The arguments in our home were frightening throughout my childhood, and usually I thought he was at fault and had treated my mother horribly. Nonetheless, he remained at home and actively cared for us while we were growing up. I learned as an adult that such perseverance was also a form of love.

The Wedding Night

My mother told me the story of her horrific wedding night when I was fully grown. It was proof that her married life had been horrible from the start. Although I don't doubt or excuse the incident, I'm amazed that love can survive such trauma.

Verbal Combat

My mom's verbal jabs and assaults also probably triggered my dad's temper. She regularly referred to her superior education and interest in current events, which was enhanced by her habit of reading and her constant attention to the news.

"You're just an ignoramus – you're a round-headed fool," she would often shout.

Their arguments ranged from petty issues to important ones. As a young child, I understood his point that I didn't really need the two Easter outfits she'd purchased for me one year. As a teenager, I saw that those major battles over household bills and later, concerning which college my brother would attend, had more to do with control than money. My parents were a study in the competition and jealousy that can undermine marriage.

Chapter 7

The Striver

After several years of marriage, the only thing my mother wanted more than a Howard University degree and a successful career was to have children. She'd always been drawn to the playful, loving innocence of children. More importantly, she wanted to shape her own children to achieve the kind of success too often beyond the reach of most Black people. So, the arrival of a son after ten years of waiting and praying marked a new beginning for her.

With the end of the Second World War and the start of America's baby boom, motherhood was viewed as the natural lock-and-key to ease women out of the workforce and, happily or not, again tie them to the home. For my mother, however, motherhood was a springboard instead of a trap tying her to an expected role in life. She had always worked and wanted to continue to earn money to push her children to a new level. She was determined to give us, she would explain as we grew up, the finer things of life.

Nonetheless, my mom said she felt uneasy about the future in those early years.

She was determined to provide her baby son with the best of everything but wasn't sure if my dad would agree to pay for the extra lessons and experiences she wanted for him. She decided that building her own financial security and independence would be the best way forward.

Her first move would be to hold on to her marriage – despite her husband's transgressions. She admitted in later years that she continued to love my dad, but she also wanted to work again and save most of her money to create her own stepping-stone in life. A divorce, she thought, given the prevailing social attitudes, would only complicate her life. My mother's pride and independence became even clearer to me as I grew up. When talking about this phase of her life, she told me she felt a woman should "never need to ask a man for twenty-five cents to buy a box of Kotex pads."

Fortunately, she was in the right place at the right time.

Ever since Henry Ford began developing the auto industry decades earlier, Detroit had been a place for strivers like the Osbornes and the Saddlers. The drive for good jobs and fair treatment was particularly strong after the Second World War.

At family gatherings, all the talk was about how now was the time for Blacks to move forward.

Black soldiers had been a brave and critical part of the nation's success in the war.

The Tuskegee Airmen, the first African American aviators in the U.S. Army Air Corps, had flown more than 15,000 sorties in Europe and North Africa, saving many more bombers from enemy fire than other squadrons.

The all-Black 761st Tank Battalion, called the Black Panthers, distinguished themselves at the horrific Battle of the Bulge and suffered heavy casualties fighting Nazis at the Belgian and French border with Germany in 1944 and 1945.

Thousands of Black soldiers were part of the invasion at Normandy on D-Day, and thousands more fought on the Pacific islands of Saipan and Okinawa as my father did.

And yet, most of Black America also felt uneasy about the future even as their prospects should have been getting better.

Blacks saw their hopes of a new era of opportunity turn to bitter frustration. The skill and bravery of the Tuskegee Airmen and other Black soldiers were rarely acknowledged, and Black veterans were often attacked when they returned to their communities. They were sometimes beaten and jailed in the South for refusing to move to the back of a bus or arrested for "impersonating" soldiers or officers when wearing their uniforms. An explosion that became the civil rights movement was on the horizon.

Ironically, the next racial battles would be fought on baseball diamonds.

Jackie Robinson began his rookie season with the Brooklyn Dodgers on April 15, 1947, breaking the color barrier in the nation's favorite sport, and one in which players from the Negro Leagues had long excelled.

While the men of the family huddled around radios, marveling that Jackie Robinson was "fightin' the race war for all of us on baseball diamonds," my mom said she had her own concerns and made her move.

"Hey dear," she said, intentionally catching her husband while he was distracted and in a good mood as he listened to a baseball game. "You know we were able to get the house and do a lot more because I was working during the years before the war and before the baby. And of course, you're moving up with your new job now. But I plan to look for something part-time to give me a little money for a new dress, and for our little one, okay? I'll let you know if I find anything good."

"Sure, Dutchess, that's not a bad idea, even though it'll be hard to do," he replied, without turning his attention from the radio.

So, when Darryl was just eight months old, my mom found a part-time job working a few afternoons and evenings in a small factory and got both my dad and Rick to commit to caring for the baby while she worked.

The plan collapsed after several weeks. She returned home one evening to find her baby feverish and crying. She said Dad had left the house, and Rick was practicing his trumpet with his bedroom door closed.

Enraged to find her baby neglected, she screamed, "You mean I can't even trust you to watch your own son and brother for a few hours? What good are you guys anyway?"

Despite their apologies, my mom realized the men of the family couldn't be trusted with her most precious possession. She quit her new job and resigned herself to having less than she'd hoped for.

As her anger cooled, my mother found something to celebrate. Rick had won admission to Wayne State University in Detroit and would major in music. She claimed the news as a victory because she had preached the importance of higher education while Rick finished high school in Detroit.

"A college degree will give you so many choices, Rick! You might one day have big jobs that will take you far away from Detroit and Alabama," she'd told him. "Don't give up and jump into a factory job after high school."

Most of the time, Rick wasn't paying attention to the lectures. A tall, handsome boy with our dad's charming smile, he enjoyed playing practical jokes on Dad and his stepmom. He was happy to have his dad in his life – something he'd missed as a small boy in Alabama – even though he complained about his father's insistence that he complete a never-ending list of chores.

On weekends and after his classes at Wayne State, the dutiful stepmother listened closely to Rick's trumpet solos while taking care of Darryl and giving him his bottle. She would then request a soft lullaby as she put the baby down for a nap.

"I know you know about our great musicians, Louis Armstrong, of course, and Duke Ellington and Count Basie, but I also want you to know about the great writers and politicians who are making a way in the world for young guys like you," Mom said. "Mark my word - you're too smooth and sophisticated for factory work. That horn and a degree could really take you a long way."

Many years later, Rick would often gratefully acknowledge the impact my mom's intense focus on education had on him and the trajectory of his career. After a few years at Wayne State, he was drafted into the Army. He soon learned his musical talent and education were of special interest to the Army which was sending bands to entertain troops and local populations across Europe after the war.

Along with serving in Army bands across Germany and the U.S., Rick had the opportunity to continue his musical education with well-known brass musicians including Mel Broiles of the New York Metropolitan Opera and the West Point Band and John Coffey of the Boston Symphony Orchestra. He met his wife, Hannelore, in Germany. Rick, Hanna and their three children, Susan, Richard, and Yvonne, returned to Detroit over the years when possible as his career progressed rapidly.

A few months later, my mother realized that another baby was on the way. Because my birth resulted in her second delivery by Cesarean section – which was still considered a major operation in 1950 - she happily accepted support and help at home from Cassie Winters, her best friend from Tilden Street AME, who shared my mom's sharp wit, intelligence, and determination to do well in life.

Aunt Cassie became our godmother. A tall attractive woman with hazel eyes that seemed to immediately discern an individual's character or sincerity, Cassie usually knew of all the gossip involving marital infidelity and other transgressions throughout Detroit's West side Black community. The two young women spent long afternoons laughing and talking on days when Aunt Cassie would cook and do the laundry for her friend.

During the early years of our lives, my mom also became closer to her own mother, who now saw that her youngest daughter had married into a family focused on achievement and built the kind of stable middle class life she'd envisioned when she pushed her family to escape the South. As the grandchild who looked most like Josie Osborne, I quickly became my grandmother's favorite.

Just a few years later, Josie's heart disease worsened, and my mom spent most of her time caring for her, with little help from her two sisters in the city, Novela and Mordel. Novela continued to be estranged from her parents. With too many bad memories between them, Novela usually kept her distance from her younger sister. Mordel had joined the rest of the family in Detroit after working in Washington, DC for several years. An alcoholic, she controlled her habit while working as a maid in white households but rarely helped care for her parents.

So, Josie's last days and months were my mother's burden to bear. Depending on the weather, my brother and I were pulled in a wagon or on a sled to our grandparents' home where she took on the work of cooking, cleaning and sick care for them along with her own household chores.

My grandmother Josie passed away in the spring of 1953 as a thunderstorm drenched the city.

Years later my parents, their faces covered with solemn reverence, told me what I'd said the morning after Josie passed away.

"Mommy & Daddy, Grandma came into my room last night with rain in her hair and tried to take me away with her."

I later learned that my grandfather was devastated by the loss of the woman who had been his rock and his purpose during more than fifty years of marriage. My mom said she was also bereft at losing her mother soon after they'd developed a deeper mother-daughter bond. The loss was painful, coming just as she'd begun to ease the longing for her mother she'd experienced as a child.

As I grew up, I saw only the remaining edges of my mom's deep grief. There were stories about my grandmother's love for me, and there was my mother's touching habit of calling me 'Jeannie Jo' – adding a form of Josie's name as my middle name.

With her beloved dad, Red John, aging as well, she made sure she would make his life as easy and happy as possible. For a while, he was still working as a security guard at a factory and would eventually earn a small pension. Red John, the Osborne family's pillar of strength and integrity, was a tender, loving grandaddy to my brother and me and a regular part of our lives. The sweet apricots from the tree in his backyard were reserved just for us. He taught us to play Checkers on long summer days when both our parents were working.

"Boy – You study long, you study wrong," he'd say and puff on his pipe as he taught us the game.

My mother was accepted into Harper Hospital's Nurses Training Program when my brother had started school and I was attending a full-time nursery school program at my dad's church, Tabernacle Baptist. I later realized that my mom worked and built her own career to gain something in addition to financial security. She wanted to stay involved in the world and use her mind. That was who she was – a professional woman who maintained her professional values even when her dream of attending college seemed unachievable. She was indeed a deeply loving mother who used most of her time and money to create her children's success. The Black middle and upper classes stood on the shoulders of women like her.

But she was also a striver for her own place in the world. A striver who would make her mark on every life she touched, with little recognition.

"You're going to have a profession, get married, and have children," she often told me. "When a man comes home from a long day of doing interesting work at his office, a wife needs to be able to talk to him about more than what the baby did that day."

My Grandparents and Me

I was caught as a two-year-old, shaking a thick powder puff full of my grandmother's light brown face powder to create a delightful cloud around my head and shoulders. Lipstick and perfume came next, landing haphazardly on my face and her dresser. "You leave that baby alone – that was all out there for her anyway," came Josie's quick defense when the mess I'd made was discovered. Perfect toddler summer days were spent on my favorite gift from Josie - a green wooden swing with two seats facing each other. Rocking back and forth on my grandma's lap, I fell asleep inhaling the sweet scent of the lush pink peony bushes in my backyard.

Grandaddy Red John was the sweet, rich smell of fresh pipe tobacco mixed with old castile soap. I loved being surrounded by that comforting Grandaddy smell which was infused in his soft plaid shirts and rough denim overalls. When he settled into an easy chair, I would brush his beautiful gray hair, carefully styling the thick, silky curls around his ears and over his forehead.

Chapter 8:

Devotion

Darryl and I knew for sure that no adult was as delightful or could command the world better than our beautiful, fun-loving Mom.

There were morning bounces on the bed and hot summer afternoons made for prancing around the house in our under-pants, with cool watermelon juice dripping from baby teeth onto bare little chests. Bubble baths and backyard tents erected from old bedspreads; Don the milkman was asked to leave a quart of chocolate milk for us when we were very good; and a puppy named Rocky- these were our joyful realities. We lived in a small Black working-class neighborhood – Detroit's Old West Side in the 1950s – where children were watched over and protected by neighbors and relatives.

Our lives were also filled with frightening, disturbing contrasts. Even though our dad went on Boy Scout camping trips with my brother and attended my dance recitals, there was the time we threw apples and oranges at him to stop him from abusing our mom. The abuse we saw didn't draw blood or result in black eyes. Still, the physical intimidation – pushing and slapping during arguments – was terrifying. My brother, who Dad would sometimes punish by whipping with his belt, suffered more than I did from the trauma of our early environment.

Each year as the March winds arrived, Dad helped us build and fly kites. On a couple of trips to a lake, I learned, reluctantly, to bait a hook and fish. One December when Darryl was very young, he accidentally-on-purpose pulled down a fully decorated Christmas tree to prevent what he thought would be a real attack on our mom.

Amid the confusion and joy of our early childhood years, Mom was our refuge and our greatest resource.

"Aaayyy, aaayy," we screamed as a monster, her face covered in spiked towers of Pond's Cold Cream crept slowly from our small bathroom, then underneath the dining room table and toward the living room where we were watching television.

Our mom's way of making bedtime fun.

Later at a Boy Scout picnic in sun-dappled River Rouge Park ....

"Would any of you mothers like to race these strong ten-year-old boys?" the scoutmaster said. "Oh – okay Mrs. Saddler – I was just kidding; you really don't have to. . .

"And the winner is -- Darryl's mom, Mrs. Saddler!"

"And the winner of the re-match is – Mrs. Saddler!!

On Thanksgiving Day, our family, loaded with doughnuts and hot chocolate, watched Detroit's big Christmas parade. By the time Santa Claus and his sleigh arrived on Woodward Avenue, the city's main downtown street, Mom had already planned her tour de force of holiday joy.

She spent her precious days off from work driving Darryl, our friends, and me to the Ford Motor Company's Rotunda – a large domed building in suburban Dearborn which was transformed each year into a Christmas wonderland of decorations and bobbing, motorized elves and puppets. Santa, of course, sat on a throne at the top of a gigantic winding staircase where hundreds of enthralled children awaited their visit with him.

On Christmas Eve, our real Santa was a nurse who worked the midnight shift. During her lunch break, she'd guide her sleigh home to silently place her hidden bounty - toy trains, baby dolls and bicycles - among twinkling Christmas tree lights and half-eaten cookies.

All to earn shrieks of delight at dawn.

Our mom also easily conquered both physical and emotional traumas. When Darryl was struck by a car a half block from our home and suffered a triple leg fracture, Mom and Dad sprinted to his side when neighbors told them of the accident. When the ambulance arrived, Mom entered the vehicle and gave strict orders without shedding a tear.

"I'm a nurse at Harper Hospital and this boy's mother. You had better drive us directly to that hospital where I can get a surgeon to save his leg. Receiving Hospital (then the city's public hospital) can't handle this. You just drive now, or I'll take him myself."

In a different, but very emotionally important way, my mother ensured that the brutal focus on colorism within the Black community never bruised my ego, despite my deep brown complexion. Elementary school classmates sometimes derided me as "black" for getting perfect grades. Once I overheard an aunt say that it was good I had long hair if "she had to be so black."

Mom fought back with her trademark brand of humor and ridicule.

"People who talk that talk are just dumb, ugly, and tired of looking like death eating a soda cracker," she would say. Guffaws of laughter followed that line. "And they really just want to look as good as you and me!"

Because of my mother's constant focus on intelligence and achievement, I soon learned to regard comments about skin color as something used to hide an individual's insecurity. She taught me that lighter-skinned people were also hurt by the tired, dull weapon of colorism, and were often more eager for all Black people to let it go.

In many ways, my family life in those years settled into an even pattern. Mom began spending most of her salary on the extras for us. We had piano, ballet, and tap-dancing lessons that few other Black children of that era enjoyed.

Darryl also provided a healthy dose of mischief in those days. By his seventh-grade year at St. Benedict the Moor, our Catholic elementary school, Darryl was at his most creative. He bought itching and sneezing powder at a small penny arcade shop and took the products to school.

"Sister, sister, can I please go to the bathroom and wash up?" a boy said as he ripped off his maroon tie and scratched his neck and arms through his tan uniform shirt. "Darryl got some on me!"

Sr. Mary Jovita, a stern member of the School Sisters of Notre Dame, an order devoted to educating Black children, laughed as she told our mother about the prank in a meeting. Nonetheless, a "D" for Darryl's quarterly grade in conduct followed, along with the expected punishment at home. Away from his hearing, however, teachers, parents, and many kids, were laughing.

It was the early 60s and a kid's prank was the only comic relief in many Black communities around the country. For many years, our mother Thelma had been reluctant to take us to Alabama to visit our paternal grandparents, remembering her own harrowing experiences as a young child in the Jim Crow South. In 1955, the horrific murder of Emmett Till, the fourteen-year-old Chicago boy killed in Mississippi, transformed her fears into a permanent edict. And when Emmett's mother decided to allow photographs of her son's deformed, mangled body to appear in Jet Magazine, many Black parents around the country temporarily made the same decision. But unlike a generation of Black children from Northern cities who later often traveled South to visit family, we were never taken on such trips after the Till murder.

The civil rights movement – complete with the police beatings of the Freedom Riders and the fire hoses set upon marchers – would only come into our lives on evening television news programs. I was frightened and transfixed.

"Dr. King gets my respect for what he's doing," my mom would declare in family discussions, "but I must agree with Malcom X! I would never let those crackers beat me up like that."

Dad, who had grown up near Birmingham, where Sheriff Bull Conner beat protestors mercilessly, knew that for too many years, death was the price of any direct defiance.

"Things got to change somehow; King and them are doing the right thing, now that they got some national newspaper and TV reporters down there," Dad said.

I saw his face cloud with anger once again, at the thought of nearly dying in war for a country that still was a threat to his children.

"You kids keep your studies up. There could be a huge change for the better for our people soon."

Memories of the injustice he and other Black boys and men suffered in the South, mixed with his old nightmares about fighting in the jungles of the South Pacific, had created anger and discontent that often was directed at his family. Mom tried to avoid his rage and struggled to explain it to us as a kind of permanent nervous condition.

In good times and bad, her great plans for her children and herself never wavered. She worked the night shift at Harper, from 11 p.m. to 7 a.m. so that she could care for and watch over us.

Throughout our elementary school years, she returned home each morning in time to make breakfast and our school lunches and send us off to school. She would take a nap, and then get up to welcome us home, supervise homework and prepare dinner, before taking another brief nap to get ready to leave for work.

It was a punishing schedule, and she rarely got enough sleep. As we grew older, Mom began working at other hospitals on her days off to save money because she wanted to move to a better neighborhood.

"What did I know, what did I know/ of love's austere and lonely offices?" (Robert Hayden)

Chapter 9:
Struggle and Loss

When my parents decided to search for a larger home, they had the advantage of owning their two-family flat, so the rent from both units in that home would cover most of the mortgage for a single-family house. My mom's aggressive savings provided much of the down payment and because Dad was a World War II veteran with a good civilian job with the Army as a missile technician, he secured the mortgage through the Veterans Administration – a benefit often denied to Black veterans in that era.

There was the usual dispute about how much they could afford to spend on a property. Nevertheless, in 1960, they settled on a large brick home in Russell Woods, a quiet, leafy West Side neighborhood that had been integrated for several years, and where just a few white families remained. The home, located on Fullerton, between Broadstreet and Petoskey, was a stately structure with four bedrooms, a driveway and two-car garage, and an impressive, large living room.

Mom set about furnishing the living room and the separate dining room in the French and Italian Provincial style she had admired when she lived with Dr. & Mrs. Turner as a young girl. I enjoyed furniture shopping with my mom - lightly bouncing on each pretty sofa and sitting at glowing dining room sets - and admired her choices.

After the first floor was re-carpeted, a white brocade sectional sofa was purchased – from Kaufmann's Furniture, a respected, small concern - for one corner of the living room.

Mom chose a large gold and white lamp to sit behind the sofa, anchored by the figure of a woman in ancient Roman-esque garb with one hand cupped above her eyes and peering into the distance, the other hand seemingly guiding her young son and daughter through a storm. The image, as she would often explain to friends years later, symbolized her determination to protect her children and give them every advantage she could.

Delicate pink French Provincial chairs were selected for either side of the fireplace, with a round marble coffee table sitting between them. The cherry wood Wurlitzer piano Mom had purchased as we began piano lessons a few years earlier anchored another corner of the room and picked up the tone of an Italian Provincial dining room set. Gold brocade draperies were chosen for both rooms. She then purchased tall artificial green plants to stand in front of two rectangular side windows with leaded glass panes. Visitors frequently commented on the elegant furnishings.

Dad complained that Mom had spent far too much. He'd gone along, it seemed, with her extra spending on items for my brother and me such as private schools, piano and dancing lessons. He also knew that my mother had often simply spent her own money on things without consulting him.

So, when the final purchase for the new house was delivered – a multi-layered crystal chandelier for the dining room – he exploded. He was determined to take control.

"We're goin' out the world backwards with all this stuff, Dutchess! I'm not gonna pay for all this . . . this is on you!" he shouted. "We'll be in hock for the rest of our lives. We already have a better house and a new furnace – what else do you want? Why are you trying to be so big?"

Without hesitation, my mother shot back.

"You just don't know how to live the right way. This is what a home should look like. I'm not gonna live here with it lookin' like an empty barn - I don't care what you say!"

"I know you don't care, but I'll make you care!" Dad growled angrily. "I ain't paying for this – we could be losing everything and out of this house soon."

Doors slammed and the argument raged. Darryl and I shuddered with thoughts of real fights we'd seen between our parents as younger children. In those days, we didn't know what the arguments were about, just that we felt the danger and saw our mother's tears. As we settled into a much larger home and a better neighborhood, we'd hoped our family life would enter into a more peaceful pattern. It was not to be.

With her back against the wall, I could see the frustration and anger on my mom's face. To my surprise, however, the argument ended that evening. The next day, she suggested a plan for the house she guessed would appeal to him more than furniture for the living and dining rooms.

" Hey Duke – why don't we make the big basement into a tiled and paneled recreation room, complete with a bar and a ping pong or pool table? If you'll pay for that – just leave the rest of the furniture payments to me."

Dad liked the idea of a bar for entertainment and agreed, ending the dispute. I remember the slightly sarcastic sneer that appeared on the side of his face indicating, in my view at the time, that he went along with the plan mostly because he thought Mom wouldn't be able to pay for the fancy furniture she'd bought on credit by herself.

The deal intensified the long-standing conflict in their marriage regarding family finances. In the early years of their union, according to my mom, they argued about suspicions of

Dad's infidelity. But because my mother had continued to work throughout most of the marriage, they were more financially secure than most Black couples. Even though she continued to insist on controlling the money she was earning, I believe my dad felt he had the right to control major decisions and purchases.

Mom continued to work her main job at Harper Hospital, and on her two off days, she took on positions at the Jewish Home for the Aged and Lakeside General Hospital to pay for the furniture and buy the other items she wanted for the home and for us. Soon they began to divide the household bills and pay them separately.

"I'm robbin' Peter to pay Paul," she'd say as she sat at the dining room table, writing check after check to make whatever payment she could afford on her purchases.

My stomach would tighten as I saw worry lines covering my mother's face. There was indeed a price to be paid.

One Saturday during an August heat wave in the city, Mom returned from an extra nursing home job and sat on the steps leading to the newly installed recreation room to watch us happily playing pool. I ran to welcome her home with hugs and then hurried back across the room where I was trying to beat Darryl at a game. As I balanced my cue stick in place, I looked up and saw my mom suddenly slump unconscious, even though she was seated at the time.

"Dad, Dad – come quick! Mom is hurt," we both screamed, terrified.

After reviving her with a cold washcloth, Dad led Mom up to bed, where she eventually seemed to recover with rest.

"Your old Mom is okay," she reassured me when I brought iced tea and cookies to her bedside. "Just a little sip of tea and she's up and going again," she said, lifting a tight fist and arm as if she was Super Woman about to take flight. "All I need is my little girl; thank-you baby."

Mom could see that we were worried about her but wasn't able to reassure us. Many nights, when she backed out of the driveway ready to head downtown to work the night shift at Harper, she would look up and see me go-go dancing in front of my bedroom window that overlooked the driveway, hoping for a smile. Darryl, always the family comedian, could make mom double-over with laughter while preparing dinner.

"Bang, zoom! To the moon," he'd say, mimicking old episodes of "The Honeymooners" with Jackie Gleason, or other situation comedies our mother enjoyed.

Despite those efforts, quite often the antics stopped and we swallowed our laughter when our dad entered a room or arrived at the dinner table.

A few times, arguments raged and there was the fear of the unimaginable.

"I should just slap you into hell right now! You gonna quit tryin' to boss me and my money around," I heard my dad growl.

Dishes shattered and chairs slammed around the kitchen, the sounds competing with the warm scent of coffee, fried eggs and toast.

"Naw - you're the low-down, cheatin' coward everybody thinks you are – just playing big-time and spending all your money on cheap women. I just wish my dad and my brothers were here to beat your ass," my mom wept as she spat out words to counter what I feared was a physical fight.

I was twelve years old.

Still in my pajamas, I dashed down the back stairs leading to the kitchen. I bent down low and then wrestled my way between my parents to face my father with his arms raised and with tears flowing down my cheeks. The attack suddenly disappeared. Dad quickly left through a side door, swearing and sweating, and started his long drive to the Army base where he worked. Mom hugged me for a while as we both cried. She then insisted I go back to bed to calm down before the school day.

Darryl slept through the storm that I will never forget. I knew my mom was doing everything possible to ensure her son wouldn't learn how bad things were and try to defend her. We both knew dad was always quick to whip Darryl but never turned his temper on me.

My brother always sent me to ask our dad for pocket change to buy candy or ice cream, knowing it was our only hope for success. I remember only one light spanking from my father, that ended almost as quickly as it had begun. Occasionally he would snap at me in annoyance. However, he would beam with special pride at my perfect report cards. He failed to notice what I knew – that Darryl's grades, which were almost as good as mine, were earned with very little effort.

For years, Dad's manner had rocked between jovial, even happy, and a dark outrage. He would lose control and want to fight over the funny but belittling insults our mom often delivered.

I wondered – where was the daddy who waltzed his six-year-old daughter around the huge, polished dance floor on the ferry boat headed to the Bob-Lo Island amusement park on the Detroit River?

Where was the father who happily took his kids sledding and helped them fly kites? What had happened to the dad who carried his big thermos full of hot chocolate when we attended the city's Thanksgiving Day Parade?

Even though there had been many good times, Darryl and I learned to give Dad the kind of wary deference required, while hiding deep fears and confusion. Mom tried to explain Dad's behavior by referring to the story of Frankenstein, saying he was a "Dr. Jekyll and Mr. Hyde." She also insisted that no matter what happened, we must always treat him with the utmost respect, quoting the biblical commandment to 'honor they father and mother.'

After the horrific fight, my parents continued living separate lives in the same house, leaving their arguments, I assumed, until the moments when we were away.

A few months later, Mom took on more responsibility as Grandaddy's health declined, and it became clear that once again, none of her brothers or sisters were willing to help care for their parents.

Mom moved Grandaddy into the back bedroom where he spent his final months. My brother and I would take his dinner to his bedside – not knowing what to say or do as the coughing and moaning overtook him. Sometimes, I would gently brush his hair and read to him until he fell asleep. When Mom was nearby, he would press together four fingers on his right hand, a gesture he adopted to indicate that his youngest daughter and her children were the closest people in the world to him.

On a raw November evening, Mom came home from a nursing home job and heard her dad emitting a loud, raspy breathing pattern and moaning – a sound often termed a "death rattle" at the hospital. She rushed to his room to find him nearly unconscious and quickly called an ambulance. Still in her white nurse's uniform, she drove to the hospital behind the ambulance. Mom later explained that she had paced and prayed for nearly an hour outside the small room in the emergency department until the doctors revived him and finally called her to his side.

"There's my baby," she said Grandaddy had cried out to her as he struggled to lift himself from the bed a final time.

He was weaker than she'd ever seen him, a shadow of the man who had always stood between her and trouble if she would just call him. Mom said she then hugged him tightly and felt life sweep out of him and surround her.

As she eased his head back onto the hospital gurney, she saw between their loosened embraced, her dad's hand pressed to his heart – four fingers held tightly together.

After returning home by herself, Mom sat slumped on the sofa in tears and loneliness. Darryl curled into her side, and I stretched across her lap, caressing her legs as she stared out at the freezing cold day.

Later that night, she listened to a favorite sad ballad recorded by Dinah Washington, "This Bitter Earth." She felt the world was indeed a hostile place without her beloved dad. She wondered if she could keep the courage and the drive burning in her soul without the one who had been their source, the one who had supported all her dreams.

I watched my mother somehow hold her deep grief at bay and move on to honor her father, Red John Osborne.

In the coming days, the house filled with aunts, uncles, and cousins that I hadn't seen in years. Relatives, neighbors, and friends arrived - in the African American tradition – with baked hams, and chickens as well as cakes and pies. Soon, teenaged cousins, happy to get acquainted again at long last, were dancing to Motown hits in the recreation room.

"I'm sorry everybody's acting like they're at a party, Mom," I apologized as I helped her serve the visitors, who were doing more socializing than comforting.

"That's okay, baby. I know you kids loved Grandaddy. Now we have to live like he wanted us to live," she said. "Just let me get these old folks out of here. They think he had some money for them to inherit but he only had his little house. I'll let them have that. We have your granddaddy's strength and spirit and his love."

Mom kept only her father's favorite pipe, a soft red flannel shirt, and a treasured silver dollar dated 1888 he found lying on the ground at a South Carolina farm where he'd worked as a young boy. It was his good-luck piece.

In a country where Red John and many other proud but poor Black men and women had navigated the Great Migration to the

North, the luck and the hope inspired by the early civil rights marches seemed to – once again – slip through their outstretched hands.

The stunning assassination of President John F. Kennedy in 1963 was, for the entire nation, a trauma that would mark an end to the comfortable idea of America the all-powerful. As the terrorism against African Americans continued in the South and the brutal, high-profile murders that marked the civil rights movement followed - the assassinations of Malcolm X in 1965, of Dr. Martin Luther King, Jr. and Robert F. Kennedy in 1968 - Black Americans knew their lives were, as always, in the crosshairs of a violent nation.

The greatest pain: Black boys and men were being snatched up to fight a war in Vietnam that had never threatened their lives like injustice in America.

"Not my son; not MY son - he won't be caught in President Johnson's war machine," Mom would often say.

Soon, uprisings against many injustices – termed riots – erupted from city to city.

Detroit suffered one of the worst uprisings in 1967.

Despite and because of her lingering grief at losing her dad and her fear of a new era, Mom became even more actively involved in protecting us and preparing us for the future. Our teen years continued to proceed according to her plans.

'BOT-de-da-de-DA. . . . BOT-de-da-de-DA' -- were the hot, happy rhythms of the Boogie Woogie Jam that jumped from Darryl's piano practice session after Mom found a new teacher, local jazz musician, Hal McKinney, who moved easily between Beethoven, Bach, Miles and Bird.

"Sachay, pa de chat, arabesque -across the floor, girls!" – came the exacting orders from my ballet teacher, Mrs. Taynton, who presided over my classes three times each week. During rest breaks, young ballerinas turned up their radios to prance around to the sound of "*Dancin' in the Street*"by Martha Reeves and the Vandellas.

At home, with Mom as the satisfied chaperone, joy and playfulness were always present. The house was a welcome haven for our friends who could face so much danger beyond the confines of our home.

We danced or played pool in the recreation room and boys used a backyard hoop to master their basketball moves. For the most part, these teenagers weren't the super-privileged off-spring of the city's Black doctors and lawyers. Like the Saddlers, their parents had solid jobs supported by the city's strong industrial economy – as nurses, government and factory workers – that sustained intact families with hopes and dreams for their children. Few of those parents, however, pursued every experience and advantage for their young ones as aggressively as my mother.

Following our mom's lead, Darryl and I campaigned to help elect Detroit's impressive young candidate, John Conyers, Jr., to the U.S. House of Representatives. Conyers had been a college classmate of two nephews on the Saddler side of the family. He was one of the many progressive politicians she would support and applaud over the years.

So, as the country fell apart, Mom put together her children's lives. The lessons weren't always easy ones. When my high school, Our Lady of Mercy, a private, mostly white Catholic girl's school, moved to suburban Farmington, she strictly instructed me to find an empty lunch table in the cafeteria on the first day at the new school and sit by myself.

"Let those girls come sit with you; they're lucky to be in classes with you, not the reverse!" she ordered. And when Darryl was crushed at failing to make the basketball team at the Jesuits' University of Detroit High School, she reacted with certainty. "We have more than enough Negro athletes and actors; there are better things in store for you."

Soon, our family was watching the 6'2" young man strut his stuff with the marching band, swinging his clarinet back and forth before football games.

Chapter 10:

Not My Son

The air was still warm, and the moon glowed that night, after a glorious Indian summer day, as I watched my mom back out of our driveway and head to work at Harper via the Lodge Freeway. She'd commented earlier that without question, fall was her favorite time of year, full of the beautiful red and gold oak, elm and maple leaves that crowned the Midwest. She even welcomed the smoky scent of the leaves her neighbors had raked and burned earlier that day.

I often wondered if she longed for company on those dark, late-night drives to work in the sturdy yet stylish Chrysler 300 my parents had purchased. But whenever I asked about those solo journeys, she would say they gave her a chance to reflect on life and plan her next steps, while she was between the duties of home and the pressures of work. I could recall only a few times when my parents went out socially when we were very young, but most of her time was consumed by planning for holidays, family gatherings, and school activities for my brother and me. She had only a few close friends in her life - my godmother, Aunt Cassie, and one or two longtime nursing colleagues.

Wearing her starched white nurse's uniform, with her cap pinned "just-so", among freshly pressed black curls that framed her large brown eyes, my mom would set off for work.

She knew the parents she missed so deeply would be proud of her achievements. Before her beloved Dad, Red John, closed his eyes a few years earlier, he mentioned on several occasions that he "gloried in her spunk" – because of her profession, her beautiful home, and in the nearly perfect lives of his two youngest grandchildren.

With her job secure, Mom hoped she could relax and enjoy life a little more. Darryl was enjoying his second year at Michigan State University – even though Dad said he should live at home and attend Wayne State University in the city to save money. Once again, Mom stepped in and, wanting her son to enjoy the campus experience he hoped for, said she would pay his tuition on her own.

My mother must have spent time on those drives deciding how to transform us into responsible, college-educated adults. Both of us were, she often said, "so spoiled you wouldn't be good to eat." She thought we weren't ready for a cruel world. In fact, our parents had told us very little about what Black people had endured in the South for generations. We assumed the discrimination that clearly still existed would be gone for good by the time we were adults.

Mom's directions for me were hard and clear.

"It doesn't matter if he's Officer Friendly or Rev. Father So and So -- a man, is a man, is a man and don't you trust him," she'd often say.

And - "You're going to have a profession and a husband and children, she advised. "But a woman always must guard and protect her reputation. A man can roll around in dirt but when he gets up and puts on a clean shirt, he's still Mr. So and So. That's not true for women."

My mother's edicts would emerge easily when she deemed a particular lesson appropriate - with a slight frown or a laugh on her beautiful movie star face. More importantly, she shared her beliefs with the certainty and support of Gospel, enlivened with examples from real life or literature.

The road map for Darryl was more difficult. "You don't want to be out there with no education, digging ditches," she warned, as she kept the prospect of college and the professions in front of him. He was her biggest worry. No amount of tough-love advice and encouragement would be enough to keep him out of the jungles of Vietnam. He was already registered for the draft. Every day it seemed, hundreds of young men, a large share of them from Black communities, had their lives upended to join the fight against the small communist country.

However, our brother Rick, who was drafted in 1952, was building a great military career as an Army bandmaster.

He eventually became the bandmaster and conductor of the highly regarded 298th Army Band (Berlin Brigade) which was famous for connecting with the German people when their country was divided by communism. At various times in his career, he also led army bands across the U.S., and as a Chief Warrant Officer, often was chosen to entertain top U.S. officials.

With his career going so well, my parents knew there was no way that Rick could influence his brother's draft status. In fact, Rick was the band master for the 1st Cavalry Division Band that provided music for troops in Vietnam. Known as a "combat band," the soldier-musicians carried M-16 rifles as well as their instruments. They often had to drop their instruments and pick up their M-16s to join a fire fight at the edge of the jungle. I remember my family huddling around the television in amazement when Rick's band was featured on the *CBS Evening News with Walter Cronkite.*

Arriving at work and turning into the hospital parking lot after her drive full of thoughts and planning, my mom said she hoped to be able to put aside her worries.

Within her work environment, she'd earned something more valuable to her than her uniform revealed – the respect of her peers and the recognition of her skills by the hospital's top doctors and officials.

Sometimes over family dinners, my brother and I learned that our mom was the nurse entrusted with the care of VIP celebrities and politicians. She'd cared for a former Michigan governor as well as other notable figures and also for Motown great Stevie Wonder.

She was also the nurse who could be called to assist a doctor during emergencies. We were amazed when she told us about the time she was on duty in the emergency room and had to assist a doctor who tried to save a patient's life with a risky procedure, even as the man had begun to bleed profusely. Fortunately, mom said she was able to maintain her composure and her grip on the man's torso. The unfortunate patient didn't survive. Nonetheless, her skill during that blood-soaked effort became legendary among her peers.

She was also known for making routine care easy to accept. She could insert a needle into arms or buttocks gently while distracting patients with light humor or telling them about her own family. And in an era when nurses had to count the narcotic medications allotted to each floor after each shift, it was Nurse Saddler who was most trusted with the important duty.

Mom's standing at the hospital also won her respect from relatives, who would ask her advice on health issues. If they were admitted to the hospital, they looked forward to her occasional visits and extra attention.

So, my mother's revelation to me -- of how she handled the most difficult challenge of her life – began with the story of just such a routine visit. Although she was in her late 80s at the time, she remembered and recounted clearly how she overcame that challenge.

She arrived at work early one evening to visit a cousin who had been admitted for a surgical procedure under the care of a gynecologist she'd recommended. Walking at her usual rapid, almost military pace, Mom breezed past colleagues at the nurse's station on the floor devoted to gynecological care, explaining that she was on her way to visit a relative before her shift began on her regular floor.

"Hey Lula – how're you doing tonight?" Mom asked, her polished white shoes coming to a full stop in the hospital room's doorway, and her voice faltering with surprise.

There, seated in a chair very close to the bed, holding the patient's hand, was Dr. Jack Washburn, a well-known Black general practitioner. Mom knew of his large practice; her husband and several of her in-laws were his patients. And she'd heard young women swoon over his good looks: wavy hair, broad smile and twinkling hazel eyes. Mom said she'd never liked him much, sensing in his manner more narcissism and well-practiced charm than professionalism. To her, his presence in Lula's room, alone and holding her hand late in the evening, certainly was a surprise.

"Oh, hey Thelma – sorry I forgot you planned to visit tonight," Lula said nervously, drawing a sheet up to her neck, but not before it revealed a gown of black lace and satin fitting loosely over an ample bosom.

"I'm sure you know Dr. Washburn. Lester and I are friends with the doctor and his wife, Kay," Lula said.

"Of course – good to see you, Dr. Washburn," Mom offered as she turned to make a quick exit. "I'll see you a bit later, Lula."

"Of course, good to see you as well," the doctor replied. "My best to your family," he added as he saw Mom rush down the dark hall.

As she approached the brightly lit nurse's station, she made the quick decision to climb two flights of stairs to the floor where she worked rather than risk running into Dr. Washburn again at the elevator.

My mother mentioned what I already knew – that she'd worked too hard during most of her adult life to keep up with the casual comments or gossip about who was cheating on whom in the community. But a connection between the debonair Dr. Washburn and her attractive, fun-loving cousin, who was married to a dull but successful owner of a dry-cleaning business, was easy to see as a match. Still, she felt bad for their children and spouses and would keep the suspicious-looking scene to herself. At the time, she later recalled, she never suspected the brief encounter would be one of the most important events of her life.

In January 1968, the apocryphal year of the mid-twentieth century, Mom's worries about Darryl's draft status took shape – as hopelessly dark, frozen and potentially deadly as the Michigan winter.

Our home was warm and full of the aroma of a favorite family dinner in the winter - a thick beef vegetable soup with homemade cornbread. I'd left the day's mail on the kitchen table for my parents and was finishing my homework. That night as Mom went through the pile of mail before leaving home for work, I heard her voice curl up the backstairs in distress. I dashed down to the kitchen and saw her leaning over the table crying, holding an envelope marked U.S. Selective Service. Dad had rushed to the kitchen as well.

"They classified Darryl 1-A," Mom said through tears. "No, no, no. President Johnson can't take my son. It'll be over my dead body – I swear!!"

My dad began to pace around nervously.

"Ah, Dutchess, I guess he'll have to do his duty. That's what we all had to do in wars for years and years..."

The mere suggestion that her son might have to fight in Vietnam brought out huge screams from Mom's gut. She turned to face her husband like a rolling volcano.

"If you won't fight this, I will. We can go to Canada, or we can go to hell. I'm not giving up my son to this damned war!"

My father had no appetite for an argument that night. His arms began to itch and he knew his skin would peel again soon from a strange infection he'd picked up in the South Pacific during World War II. The rash hadn't bothered him for years, but I assumed it had started again. He went and grabbed an old jar of cooling cream from the bathroom and then headed to his car in the driveway.

Many years later, I learned what he'd done that night after he'd talked about his distress to my husband.

After smearing the cream on both his arms and upper chest, making his light reddish-brown skin burn as he applied it, he revved up the small Dodge Rambler he always drove to work and headed through the snowy streets to the city's expressways. For nearly three hours, he drove in a trance-like state – heading away from the city – toward his job at Selfridge Air Force Base, and toward my private high school in Farmington. He even headed north toward East Lansing where Darryl was at Michigan State University and unaware of his peril, before he turned back home.

During the drive, he heard again the awful sounds of war.

Rat-a-tat-tat- tat! Pop-pop – pop-pop-pop – aargh! Spit out the mud – they're all along the sides of the road full of mud, slop, blood and biting bugs. Gotta keep pushing to get this tank back to my base, he thought.

Even on that freezing winter night in Detroit, he said he could feel once again the terror and taste of war in the muddy, hot jungles of Saipan and Iwo Jima.

Dad never told Darryl or me anything about fighting in the jungles of the South Pacific while we were growing up, but the memories had poured out of him years later in a discussion with his son-in-law who loved history and whose own father had stormed Omaha Beach on D-Day. Like most veterans, he hoped his son's generation would escape the terror of war.

He'd thought it was enough to keep his kids away from the racial targeting Blacks faced in his home state of Alabama.

Sometimes during the war, Dad recalled in that rare conversation, he heard again the snarling dogs of the South on the hunt for Black men. He and his brothers had escaped just ahead of the Klan – when their white contemporaries were threatened by any pride they displayed as young men. The murder of fourteen-year-old Emmett Till hit very close to his memories of his first home just outside of Birmingham, where his father ran a successful small charcoal business. And just a few years earlier, Medgar Evers, also a veteran, was murdered outside his home in Jackson, Mississippi for leading a voting rights campaign as head of the NAACP.

The "Double V Campaign" -- the idea that Black soldiers were fighting for victory abroad over the Nazis and victory at home against terror and segregation -- hadn't worked out well for Black soldiers. There was no reason to think service in Vietnam would somehow improve things for the race.

Dad knew that his son Darryl knew nothing of deep, down to your gut fear; of the fight to survive either a world war or home-grown hate. He'd taught him he could never drive through Dearborn – the suburb where police officers were most likely to target and arrest him. And Darryl had learned enough about his environment to steer clear of the mean or just clueless white boys at his private school to get safely to graduation.

After learning of Darryl's 1-A draft status, Dad returned home around midnight, determined, I thought, to do what he could to change his son's fate.

For weeks and months, I stood in the middle of the storm, helpless and afraid for my brother.

Mom decided to act the next morning. She called Rep. John Conyers who she'd worked to elect. He was a college friend of her favorite nephew and now was the time to get him to focus on that connection.

Frantic yet determined, she hoped Conyers could at least slow down the process. Of course, she hoped Dad could get a spot for Darryl in the state's National Guard, but feared his induction would happen only after every wealthy white kid got in.

"Hello, I'm Thelma Saddler, one of the best campaign workers for Congressman Conyers and I very much need to schedule an appointment with him. Yes, I understand he's very busy. But you must give him my name. I really must speak with him. It's about the draft. I'll call again tomorrow."

At nineteen, Darryl was paralyzed by the thought of going to fight in a war halfway around the world. He wasn't even ten years old when Dad helped him aim and fire an old Army rifle through a thick canopy of trees and toward the sky as they stood on the top porch of our old house on New Year's Eve.

Darryl never had any serious fights with his childhood friends. He was the daring kid who brought itching and sneezing powder to school one day. He was the smart kid who earned good grades with little effort. He was the only one in his class at our all-Black Catholic elementary school to win admission to one of the most prestigious high schools in the city. His time at the University of Detroit High School had been tough and dull until he bonded with the few other Black kids there.

Michigan State had become the very best experience of Darryl's young life. He loved the school's huge, beautifully designed campus in East Lansing, ninety miles north of Detroit. There were enough Black students on campus to support chapters of all the major Black fraternities and sororities, and he'd pledged and was already a popular member of Alpha Phi Alpha.

He was paralyzed by the news that he'd lost his student deferment and could soon be fighting in a war he didn't understand.

By the end of January 1968, it was clear there was no slowing down the war's brutal killing machine. The Tet Offensive – the

North Vietnamese's costly but brilliant move from guerilla warfare to directly attacking South Vietnamese and American forces across the country with about 85,000 soldiers – began on January 31 with a surprising ferocity.

Before the Tet, which was named and planned to coincide with Vietnam's traditional New Year's celebration, most Americans thought the war was at a stalemate. To General William Westmoreland, the commander of all American forces in Vietnam, progress was measured by the body count – and it was clear that thousands more Vietnamese communists were dying than American soldiers.

General Westmoreland had started his career at a South Carolina military academy – The Citadel – and then gone on to graduate from West Point. He made a name for himself during World War II, leading troops in Northern Africa and Europe.

To Westmoreland and his generation of military leaders, casualties were just the unfortunate cost of war, to be paid by the unfortunates.

Nonetheless, after Tet, American casualties: [including injuries and death] rose to more than 500 each week.

Even if many more of the communist enemy continued to die, the North Vietnamese generals had found a way to deliver a psychological blow that turned the war in their favor.

The bold Tet Offensive hit the country's capital – Saigon – including the outer walls of the U.S. Embassy. The North's forces also captured and controlled for a time Vietnam's ancient capital and cultural center, Hue.

A second phase of the Tet began in May and a third in August, altogether targeting five major Vietnamese cities, dozens of military installations, and scores of towns and villages. Although the attacks were repelled, their intensity convinced Americans that their sons were dying in a war the country couldn't win and shouldn't continue fighting.

The news of American deaths in the jungles of Vietnam - so many of them young Black men whose families had no way to keep them out of the war - felt to many families like a speeding locomotive headed toward their most precious possessions. More than 2,100 American boys were killed in the Tet maneuver alone.

I listened silently as my mother called Congressman Conyers' office at least twice a week. Because Darryl had no major health issues, the Congressman explained that winning an exemption would be difficult. He said he was taking Darryl's case, and that of many other constituents, directly to his contacts at the Office of Selective Service.

"Don't they understand – they can't just take all our boys? It's not fair; we've done enough, we've done too much for the war." Mom wept big heaving sobs on a call with a man she saw as her only hope, as her faith and hope in him was dying.

"I'm so sorry Mrs. Saddler, I'm afraid I can't do anything else," Conyers said over her sobs. "I'll make sure they take note of his eighteen months in college and hope that will get him a better assignment – something to keep him away from combat."

After that final call, Mom used cold water and light bar soap to remove stains from her Nut Brown face powder that, with her tears, had stained her nurse's uniform. Still full of desperation, she undressed and quickly ironed her stark white uniform again. Once finally ready to leave for work, she hoped the car's heater would finish drying the material her iron hadn't reached.

It was early spring in Detroit – a season barely distinguishable from winter. Daytime's stronger sunlight was the only sign of hope as it began to melt the gray-black mounds of snow and ice that lined the city's streets and expressways.

Years later, Mom told me she then decided to push down her own emotion and shock as she was trained to do during medical emergencies, to face what was certainly the bleakest moment of her life.

"I've got to make a way out of no way for my son," she whispered to herself. "I'm Red John's daughter. I must save my son."

At that moment, she knew of only one weak option and one too risky to consider. Although Dad had said he'd take Darryl down to meet with someone at the National Guard in the coming week, she feared it might be only a courtesy appointment - a slim reed to hold on to. And because the family had no connections in Canada, moving there or sending Darryl there alone to make his way was almost as risky as the war.

As Mom pulled into the hospital's parking lot for physicians and hospital staff that evening, she drove past a group of doctors she knew chatting outside in their white coats. There was Dr. Shields, a respected, well-liked surgeon, who had always been quick to compliment her nursing skills, and two other internists, Dr. Fromm and Dr. Everett, who also had been friendly to her and other top nurses. She waved as she drove past them and then happened to find a parking spot not far from the group.

It was then that she heard parts of their conversation about the war and the draft status of some boys they knew. She wasn't sure which doctor was speaking and didn't want to linger too long in her car and appear to be listening to them. But mom said she felt sure she heard one of them mention that some boys were given shots to create or enhance either allergies or diabetic tendencies.

"I didn't like that move," she remembered one physician saying clearly, "but at least the kid got a 4F medical deferment and will be able to finish college."

With her mind racing with that bit of information, she adjusted her nursing cap and hurried into the hospital's staff entrance. She now felt there might be a way to save Darryl, but she had to find the right doctor – and enough time - to make the plan work.

As she arrived at her third-floor nurse's station that night, she could tell her colleagues had been anxiously awaiting her arrival. The only obvious change in the familiar scene as the night shift nurses assembled to take the report on all patients on the floor from the afternoon shift was that the nurses' station was graced by a bouquet of long-stemmed yellow and red roses.

When the report was finished, one of the nurses who had greeted Mom with a Cheshire cat smile and raised eyebrows handed her a card.

"Hey Saddler – the flowers and this card --were delivered for you, honey! Now we bet you have got more to talk about today than your great kids! And your secret is safe with us," she added as the group scattered to check on their patients and to let the target of their suspicions read the card in private.

Mom remembered rolling her eyes and laughing at her colleagues as she started to open the envelope.

"Okay, okay . . . You girls are just looking for a laugh. I had another of those big-shot patients when I was on rotation last week, and this must be his way of saying thanks." But the beautiful card, which pictured an elaborate English rose garden, was from an entirely unexpected bigshot.

"Dear Mrs. Saddler:

I must ask you a personal favor. I hope you will agree to keep to yourself our surprise encounter when I was visiting your cousin at the hospital last week. Your kind discretion in this matter would mean the world to me.

If there is anything I can do to assist you or your immediate family in any way, please let me know.

With My Gratitude and Best Regards,
Jack Washburn, MD

Mom said her heart jumped and she began to perspire as she pushed the card into the pocket of her uniform. She began to plan and hope for a way out of no way.

Chapter 11:

Courage

There was, of course, no time to waste.

Darryl was scheduled for a pre-induction physical in just three weeks. The night Mom received the flowers and the note from Dr. Washburn as she arrived at work, she said she spent her lunch hour pacing and thinking how she might approach him for help. She walked quickly past the emergency room, matching its tension and urgency inside her own body. She paced through the psychiatric ward, One-South, hearing the shouts of confusion and misery of the mentally ill.

Finally, she stopped by pediatrics, Five-North. She looked through the huge glass window that protected the newborns connected to breathing and feeding tubes; she peeked into rooms at listless children suffering from cancer. Five-North, Mom had told us many times, was always her most difficult assignment. She found it almost impossible to lay down a suffering, sleepless baby – even if it meant she had to stay late to finish her charting for the night.

That night, Mom was holding her own child in her heart. She would take any risk and suffer any punishment if she could protect him from harm.

Any mistake, even a thoughtless misstep, could result in failure. Striking a secret and effective blow would be the only way to keep her son out of the jungles of Vietnam and away from the country's war machine.

So, as she walked, she planned to contact Dr. Washburn to take advantage of the favor he had offered if she would never mention his late-night visit to her cousin, Lula.

She would propose the price of her silence. The doctor would give Darryl a shot or some treatment to allow him to fail the medical test for induction into the Army. By posing a hypothetical question to a friend who had once served as an Army nurse, she confirmed her suspicion that testing as a diabetic would change Darryl's draft status from 1A to 4F – or medically ineligible to serve.

However, there was no reason to believe Washburn would follow through with such a dangerous favor for her. A doctor's intervention in the process could certainly cost him his medical license.

Mom had tried to think of others who might help her. There was only one Black doctor with admitting privileges and on-staff at Harper. Thelma was proud of his success, but because she didn't know him, she was sure there was no chance he would risk his status and career to help her. She also knew that Black nurses, like doctors and other professionals, couldn't risk one step across any line without paying a price. Canadian nurses from Windsor, Ontario – just across the Detroit River – were always angling for a chance to fill any opening at Detroit hospitals, which offered higher salaries than those in Windsor.

My mother had learned early in life that deception was often necessary to get through dangerous interactions with whites in the Jim Crow South. Her parents, Red John and Josie, told her that a man or woman's word and integrity were the golden elements that would fuel their own self-esteem and lift them above their peers. So, she never told anything other than "little white lies" to smooth over social situations. And she never even considered anything that would jeopardize her position at work. It was why she was the nurse most trusted to deliver an accurate count of narcotics and other medications that could be pilfered and re-sold.

Nonetheless, the bright line dividing truth and deceit disappeared when it came to the life of her precious son.

Dr. Washburn certainly had a lot to lose if his wife had proof of one of the many transgressions that had often made him the subject of gossip. He had two good-looking children, and his wife was involved in social clubs and charitable groups. They were a Black "power couple." Even if he'd grown bored with his marriage, he probably wouldn't want to relinquish his status to scandal.

She also assumed that the doctor might be able to evade her threat – and even turn it on her. Who would take a nurse's word, a woman's word, over his? What if he made a counter-threat – perhaps using his connection to the Saddler family – to ruin her marriage and reputation?

Class and status in the community was the holy grail to my mom. She hated to threaten the achievement of someone who had much of what she wanted for herself and her children. If she had achieved her dream of attending Howard University, perhaps she would be in the same social class as the doctor and his wife. She had fought hard to get into Harper's Nurses Training Program to gain not just a good job but the status she knew she deserved.

Still – status meant nothing compared to the life of her son.

Nonetheless, no matter what gossip or legal consequences might be aimed at her, she could not flinch or fail to act if she had a way to protect Darryl.

Secrecy would be her first challenge, even in her own home. Mom explained that she needed advice from someone she could trust absolutely, someone skillful and unafraid to act in a crisis.

"Duke, I feel sick to my stomach and dizzy," I heard her tell Dad when she returned from work the next morning. "I've got to take a day off. My head is pounding."

"OK, Dutchess. I know they can't say anything down at the hospital because you almost never take a sick day. You take care of everybody, so take care of yourself for a change; get some sleep," he said rushing out for his long drive to work.

I thought nothing of that brief exchange between my parents. I was happy there wasn't an argument that morning and I left to catch the school bus to my private suburban high school. Alone at home, mom said she made her first desperate phone call. She turned to her own dear friend, Cassie.

As my mom gave me the details of this dramatic story years later, Aunt Cassie's role made perfect sense to me.

"Cassie – I need your help today in the worst way," she said, her voice shaking as her friend answered the phone. "Is there any way you can come by the house today to talk? Before Duke gets home from work?"

Perhaps sensing the unusual urgency in her old friend's voice, my Aunt Cassie's reply was immediate.

"Sure, Thelma. "I'll see you in a half hour."

Few people were aware of Aunt Cassie's true value. She could see through deception and find a way through any storm. At 5'9" tall, she was what some called a handsome woman, smart and attractive at once. Her pretty smile and her twinkling brown and hazel eyes delivered warmth and sweetness handed down, no doubt, through generations. But those same eyes, when no one was looking deeply enough, told an entirely different tale.

As the youngster who for years paid close attention to adult conversations, it had always been clear to me that Aunt Cassie could quickly take the measure of men and women. The fearful question was what, if anything, she would do with what she had learned or accurately perceived. She would hold her fire and act only to protect her family and close friends. Aunt Cassie didn't suffer fools gladly. Most people only merited her disdain;

others had their punishment kept in reserve. I admired the veiled knowledge and power I sensed in my godmother.

Aunt Cassie's husband, the respected Rev. Ervin Winters, had learned his lesson early. Like so many men of the cloth, at one point he became too comfortable with his position. He had a dalliance with a woman he was sure would never come to light; one that, if it became known, was sordid enough to bar the reverend from any other good assignment. When his own hapless mistake revealed the affair to his wife, Cassie was angered and deeply hurt by the betrayal. Still, it proved to her – once and for all – that her own intuition was impeccable.

The couple remained together, but the possibility of a vengeance – best served cold - remained in the marriage and lingered in Aunt Cassie's eyes. It meant that the minister never strayed again.

Aunt Cassie might have known of my dad's rumored transgressions through her network of information at the church. But because of her love and respect for her best friend, it's unlikely she ever revealed what she knew other than with a carefully arched eyebrow or a face quickly turned away.

Mom, who was more like Aunt Cassie than most of the women in her own family, always assumed such information was available should she ever need it.

"Hey little Sis," Aunt Cassie said as she stepped into the house, finding her friend looking wearier and more worn-out than usual from her nursing shift. "What's got you so upset today?"

Over tea, Mom poured out her dilemma – Darryl's draft status – and her risky plan to keep him safe.

Was she crazy to try this? Was it too dangerous? Was there any other way?

"Tell me, Cassandra Sharp Winters, what can I do? How can I fight for my son's life and win?" Mom pleaded.

Aunt Cassie leaned back in the kitchen chair. Her familiar wry smile and the gentle spring sunlight danced across her face.

"Well, when you called me, I thought you'd finally decided to get rid of that old husband of yours," she said, reaching for a joke. "This problem with Darryl isn't an easy one. But my dear, you're not crazy. It might work. I've got two thoughts about it all."

The first approach Aunt Cassie suggested was no surprise and didn't go far beyond what Mom had decided to do. She should request an urgent appointment at the doctor's office.

She should arrive looking stern and determined. No smiling and she must skip the familiar greetings about family and friends.

Of course, she would make sure Dr. Washburn dismissed his office nurse and closed the exam room door for the appointment. Then Aunt Cassie suggested a narrative that added important details to the plan.

"Dr. Washburn, because you mentioned your willingness to help me or my family in your recent note, I'm here to say I do indeed need a favor from you. Our son has been classified 1-A in the draft and his induction physical has been scheduled in two weeks.

"As you already know, I have no interest in harming you or your family. I understand any hint of scandal is far from what you'd want. But I must ask. Will you help my son? I understand that some doctors at Harper have given relatives a shot to make them test as diabetics. Darryl is already a bit overweight."

"My word – on the lives of both my children – that neither that action, nor suspicion of anything else, will ever be revealed."

"Thanks, Cassie. I can pull that off. But what else do you have in mind?"

"Well," Cassie began. "You are so right to think that the doctor might have ways to get around your request and still gain your silence. So, I must tell you that Dr. Washburn is the chair of our board of deacons at Tilden St. AME. And – yes, there has been talk that he might have a couple of women outside of the church vying for his attention and hoping to get him away from his wife. In fact, he'd been alerted when Rev and I had that problem.

"Let me give it some thought," Aunt Cassie said. "I think I can act right away – an anonymous note of some kind might help your case. I'll let you know tomorrow, then you should make the appointment after you hear from me."

The next evening, Aunt Cassie told Mom that she had personally delivered an anonymous note to the doctor's home very early that morning and described what she imagined might have happened as a result.

There was a light clang as the small metal mailbox next to the home's front door closed. The family lived on West Outer Drive, a leafy boulevard of sprawling, brick colonial and ranch-style homes where several white families remained, living among the Black doctors and lawyers who could afford the properties.

After the family dinner was over that evening, Mrs. Washburn might have handed her husband the sealed, anonymous note addressed to him on church stationery she'd found in the mailbox that morning.

Cassie imagined that just before he retired for the night, Dr. Washburn might have remembered to look at the note.

"There may be trouble in paradise on the horizon again for our Reverend or perhaps a fellow deacon. Initials L.P. Will send more information later, through your office."

Aunt Cassie thought that perhaps Dr. Jack Washburn's gut tightened as he saw the initial L.P. He knew it wasn't necessarily an indication of something about his friend, Lula Parrish, but the coincidence was concerning. He needed to find out what was going on.

Soon after that brief call from Aunt Cassie, Mom phoned Dr. Washburn's office for an appointment.

"Late afternoon this week would be best," she said. "Yes; it's just for a quick second opinion."

* * *

She explained that she chose a matronly-looking black suit for the office visit, along with a hat with a brim to partially conceal her face. She used an old compact of pressed powder which was a shade too light for her skin to look more ashen, scared and worried, even though her face had been etched with worry for weeks. When she was dressed and ready to leave her house, she noticed she couldn't stop her underarm perspiration. She tried one more spray of Secret deodorant before leaving.

When she arrived at the doctor's office, she said she was relieved to learn her timing had been fortunate. With just two other patients in the waiting room, her wait would be relatively short. The other patients were both strangers to her.

Once face-to-face with the doctor, Mom said she began her well-rehearsed request.

"Because you mentioned an offer to help me, Dr. Washburn . . .

"Our son has been classified 1-A in the draft . . .

"I understand some doctors at Harper have given relatives a shot . . .

"My sacred word, my promise of eternal secrecy – sworn on the lives of both my children. . .

She said Dr. Washburn looked troubled, and even annoyed, remembering his last encounter with this nurse, the wife of one of his patients, who had never come to his office for care. He probably thought she was the only person he knew who had seen him in the company of Lula Parish. And he probably thought a bouquet of flowers and a personal note would be enough to secure her silence.

He'd suggested he could deliver a favor, he knew, but had in mind a small favor. Not this risky gambit.

"Do you have family members at my church, Mrs. Saddler? I thought you and your husband's family attended Tabernacle Baptist," Dr. Washburn inquired.

Mom said the doctor's usual charming demeanor had disappeared. In that moment, he was as stern and businesslike as she was. Unsure where the question might lead, Thelma decided to hide her long-ago connection to the AME church, and especially her close friendship with Cassie Winters, the assistant pastor's wife.

"Yes, the Saddlers do attend Tabernacle, but I'm a Catholic. My kids and I attend St. Benedict the Moor parish," came her reply.

It was soon apparent that even though he couldn't make a direct connection to the anonymous note placed at his home, the doctor still assumed that his marriage and position could be in danger. He continued. "As you must know, you're making a big request. Secrecy on this topic is essential. No one in your family – including your husband and children – can have any knowledge of this."

"Of course, I understand, Dr. Washburn. I understand that this can never be whispered about in any way. It will not pass from my lips.

"But his induction physical is soon – 8:30 a.m. Saturday, June 1. Is there a possibility you can assist by then?" Mom said, hoping to hide her surprise that her request would be considered and her desperation.

"Yes, I believe so, Mrs. Saddler. There is one additional warning I must add here. If word of this action leaks out and if I suffer any suspicion or consequences because of this, I will make sure that you will suffer the same – or worse. Even to the extent of bringing legal charges. Do I make myself clear?" he said.

"It is absolutely clear; you have, as I said, my promise that no one will hear of this - or anything else I might have knowledge of," she replied.

"OK. Your son must be at this office at exactly 7 a.m. on Saturday, June 1. I'll be the only one here. He shouldn't be informed of anything – not even a hint of what will happen here," the doctor again said sternly.

"He will be here for sure. Thank you for trying to help me save his life," Mom said as she gathered her purse to leave.

* * *

Darryl arrived home from MSU on a Friday afternoon after postponing one of his final exams. The drive, usually 90 minutes at most, had taken two hours as he thought about whether he'd ever make the drive to and from the university again. College, then a great job or grad school: that's what he'd been told was his future. Not a war against communists – a system he barely understood.

Little was said over dinner that night. Darryl was hoping for a miracle to keep him out of the Army; Mom was strangely quiet, praying that her secret plan would work.

"What did they say down at the National Guard post, Dad?" Darryl asked in a near-whisper.

"I'm going down there tomorrow morning, son, to get the answer," came the reply. "Hope we get good news."

Darryl already knew mom hadn't gotten help from Cong. Conyers' office. He slumped his 6'2" frame into the kitchen chair, imagining himself already on his way to basic training somewhere in the South.

"This isn't supposed to happen," he mumbled in despair. Unable to eat much of his dinner, he went to bed early, knowing he had what he was told would be a quick check-up with the family doctor, and then off to the last physical of his life.

At Dr. Washburn's office, the doctor took Darryl's temperature, weight and blood pressure, and then gave him a shot.

"Just some extra vitamins, son. You're doing pretty well. Good luck today with the Army physical."

* * *

After hours of waiting in lines to give urine samples, get blood drawn and have his reflexes tested, Darryl said he reached the final station.

"Okay Mr. Saddler. You can go now. You're diabetic and will be classified 4F," the physician told him.

Stunned and surprised, yet afraid to show it, Darryl simply said "Really?"

"Yep. Follow up with your doctor. It's a serious condition and won't work in the military."

We all rushed to the front door as my brother returned home, stunned and nervous. He announced the results of the physical to our parents, still uncertain about the diagnosis.

Mom immediately began crying and murmuring quietly to herself, "The Lord is my Light and my salvation – whom shall I fear?"

"Wait here," she ordered Darryl through her tears.

Then she nearly stumbled up the stairs to her room to compose herself and prepare to conceal her secret forever.

Chapter 12:

Memorari

Thelma & Duke

Many years after Mom saved Darryl from the draft, she told me of her conflicting emotions immediately after the heroic effort. She was thankful and amazed that he was safe, of course.

But there was something simmering beneath her joyful surface, something she couldn't name.

Because so many members of our extended family had always consulted her about health issues, everyone accepted her explanation of Darryl's "incredible luck" with his draft status. She explained that Type 2 diabetes was in her family, and she'd planned to get her children tested for it anyway.

"Thank the Lord they found it. He'll just have to watch his diet for the rest of his life."

I remember that Mom seemed more nervous in those days despite her long hours at work. Dad didn't question her mood; he was also happy with the news, and they usually retreated to separate corners of the house when they were home.

But at that time, my mother was developing a new interest in saving her own life.

She knew that on her own, she had brought her most

desperate need and hope into reality. It is one thing, she thought to herself; to say you would risk life and limb and your career to save your child. It is quite another thing to succeed. To snatch victory from the jaws of the powerful.

Her best friend Cassie, the only living soul who knew what had happened, told her the achievement wasn't a surprise.

"Oh, my little sister – with your looks and smarts, you know you've always been way ahead of everybody around you. And with a little help from this bestie and mostly your own smooth skill, there was no way to fail!"

"Truth is, Cassie," Mom said, "good looks were just handed down to me by the ancestors. And those looks never did any of us Black folks much good unless we could sing and dance or play ball. And – yes - I worked hard in school, but that skill was never tested at the highest level. So now, just between you and me, it looks like I've achieved something. Maybe there's something left for me even when the kids are grown. Thanks so much for everything, Cassie. Let's never speak of this again," she said, still in disbelief.

During my last few months at home before leaving for college, I often listened more closely than ever as my mom retold her life story. Even though at that time I didn't know anything about the accomplishment that brought all her thoughts to the surface, I began to appreciate everything I'd seen over the years and became something of a fascinated witness and confidante.

My mom was the embodiment of the old saying, "Making a way out of no way."

Her mother and dad left South Carolina, exchanging an atmosphere of terror and poverty there for a foreign, but still poor environment, in Detroit. Mom watched her parents' moves at every turn and decided she would stand on their shoulders and climb.

At just 17 – unable to make her dream of attending Howard University come true – she married and worked a series of good jobs. While my dad fought in the South Pacific during the Second World War she was, for the most part, alone, working, crying and praying.

Soon after, with her husband safely home, she mentored a stepson, brought two children into the world, and then built a career as a respected nurse.

At each stage, she would heed her dad's advice: "Root little pig or die a poor hog!"

My mother had also cared for her parents through their last days with little or no help from her siblings.

While navigating a difficult marriage, she'd saved money for down payments on two homes. There were cruel arguments and near fights with Dad at every turn, but she held on.

When he refused to pay half the cost of the elegant furnishing she chose for the second home, she took on an additional job to cover those bills. And when he shocked her by refusing to help pay their son's college tuition, claiming it was because Darryl wanted to attend Michigan State, 90 miles from Detroit, instead of living at home and attending college, she again stepped in to bear the total cost of the tuition and room and board.

Throughout my childhood, I'd been present for much of the drama, but of course, didn't fully understand it. Now, I began to worry as I saw the weight that had been on her shoulders.

Now was her most triumphant moment: My mother had used her own cunning and planning to save their son from the war that was tearing the country apart and killing so many young men.

The accomplishment had transformed her. I now understood as she sang the chorus of the old gospel song, "The Lord is my light and my salvation, whom shall I fear?"

As she reviewed her life, slowly but surely, it seemed her amazement turned into anger. She was alone with the details of a great triumph; without a mate she trusted enough to share her secret.

She was alone even in victory, with a triumph that felt hollow because no one knew of it.

She was alone just as she had been as she fought many other battles over the years.

She resented my dad for never sharing her dreams or becoming the partner she needed. Her feeling of peace became a steely determination to do something for herself.

When I left for college in the fall of 1968, my parents were 'empty nesters' with empty hearts and little in common. They both worked extra jobs to pay our school expenses, with my mom still angry that she bore all the costs for Darryl, while Dad paid my expenses that were left after the partial scholarships I won.

To pursue her long-deferred dream, Mom started classes at the local Highland Park Community College. Even though she was exhausted by her jobs, she delved hungrily into history and literature courses, earning much better grades than her young classmates.

I'd turned down admission to the University of Michigan and other colleges to join my brother at Michigan State. Despite the excitement of starting college, I worried about my mom and called home almost daily to check on her. Working and taking classes full-time, she often locked herself away from Dad in a back bedroom, where she'd study and then take sleeping pills to get some rest before going to work. It was a dangerous time.

For his part, Dad stayed away from home more often, visiting family or drinking with old friends.

I believed that in his mind, he had given up on dreams as well. Although he'd won a good job after serving in the war, his attempts to move ahead were blocked at every turn by the racist hierarchy that ruled civilian employees of the Army as well as other private and government workplaces.

At home, perhaps he faced a different battle that I couldn't see. Very rarely had Mom agreed with him or followed his lead, whether it involved their kids or their homes. I don't remember seeing them laugh together or share a knowing look or a toast during the holidays.

I blamed my dad for all the arguments, but perhaps he felt he had to give in to Mom to do what was best for us. Maybe he had vowed he'd never leave his kids without the daily protection of their own father. He had held on

Until now.

Both Darryl and I were on the way to getting our college educations and he was several years from retirement. Perhaps he wanted to enjoy life in a simple fashion and wondered if there would ever be someone who wanted the same easy life.

There was a dry vacuum in the home that easily turned any spark into a fire. Mom's fury and resentment over her lost dreams along with Dad's temper and resentment over a life with too little enjoyment. There were no kids to jump between them to prevent a physical fight; no need to protect us from hearing raging arguments.

When my mother described their last battle to me, the scene remained in my mind as real and frightening as any I'd seen.

"Now all you want to do is go to college and read all those books. You think you're just a kid again, Dutchess? This ain't no life we have here," Dad snarled one evening.

Mom, unwilling to bite her tongue, had her accusations ready.

"You're just an ignorant SOB. You don't care about learning or what's out there in the world. You just want to chase those floosies out in the street."

Then ----- threats, curses, punching and Dad leaving.

Mom said she could not, in that moment, try to appease him again, to make things last a little longer with some kind of clever compromise. Her cup was empty, save for a brief sip of kindness for herself.

The marriage lasted 33 years. Through love and striving; through war and hope. For children, despite differences. Against all odds.

But it was over.

Darryl

Darryl had always adored Mom and wanted more than anything to protect her from any kind of harm. He tried to overcome the awful storms we saw as young children.

Tears filled his eyes later in life as he remembered holding onto me as a toddler under the dining room table as our parents argued and fought.

He also had a knack for handing back to Mom the kind of joie de vivre she possessed.

"OK, Kid, now you stir up those pancakes really good," he instructed me. "When I put them on the stove, we're gonna ride our bikes down to the corner and meet Mom at the bus stop where she gets off after work!

"Hurry-up!"

Darryl carried out the plan with a rush of happiness, knowing Mom would be thrilled by the greeting party.

Indeed, the family was a delightful early morning sight – with Mom, still in her white nurse's uniform, laughing and riding my bike home as I rode on the back of Darryl's bike. When we returned home 15 minutes later, smoke was pouring from the kitchen windows. Luckily, it came from burned pancakes, not a complete fire.

Time after time, however, Mom planned Darryl's life and protected him.

It was Mom who had directed him to attend the city's best private high school. And it was Mom who insisted that he should have the chance to attend college away from home and live on a campus. My brother was a great kid - smart, personable and extremely generous. He once gave away his own used car to a poor immigrant with an expectant wife and children.

Darryl wouldn't learn how our mom had saved him from the draft until it was too late to thank her. But like so many young men in their early twenties, there wasn't the time or the inclination to look back at all the protection and love that shaped his life. He'd graduated from college. If anything, he was relieved to learn of our parents' break-up, one that seemed like it had been coming for most of his life. He wouldn't linger in sadness.

He would marry his college sweetheart and then he would attend law school. He would eventually become an attorney for the state.

Now, he was leaving home for good. He believed he would be there whenever our mom needed him.

Jeanne

My mother's rage met me at the door when I returned home one evening after visiting with my father after the divorce. As I stepped through the heavy oak door, the icy wind that had enveloped the city pushed against an equally angry force inside.

"Well did you and your father and those old catty sisters of his enjoy your day? Bad-mouthing me I'm sure," Mom said, her voice breaking.

"I didn't mean to stay so late, Mom, I'm sorry; I was just being polite," I pleaded.

I reached out quickly to hug her, but for the first time in my life, she pushed me away. I slid into a soft kitchen chair across from the woman who had made my world, who was now holding her head, her thick hair combed by worried fingers and an old robe that seemed to sit on top of layers of depression and despair. "You know I love you more than anyone in the world," I told her.

"No you don't. Where were you then?" she argued, "Just spending all your free time with the people who have always hated me the most – partly for the great way I raised my kids – beating back all comers."

After graduating from Michigan State, I began working as a reporter for *The Detroit Free Press.* Dad enjoyed taking me around the extended family to brag, and I obliged him.

"Now you're spending all your time on weekends – visiting your old cruel father and those sisters of his that hate me now," Mom exploded.

"I guess you don't want to be here with me now – the one who did everything for you all your life. The one who paid for you to spend a summer in Europe after graduation. The one who held you so close, who taught you everything, gave you and your brother every advantage – from dancing and music lessons to private schools - and now I'm here all alone. Darryl's off in law school, and you have a big job. All my 'Miss Ann of a daughter' can do is flit around the Saddlers who never cared about her until now. I guess I should just kill myself!"

I absorbed, at that moment, the waves of anger surrounding me. Tired of the constant balancing act I had endured after moving back home, my retort was unforgivable and mean.

"Well, some people would say suicide is always an option," I said.

"Et tu Brute!" Mom shot back as she left the kitchen weeping.

As I sat amazed at my own cruelty, the familiar, warm haven that was the kitchen pressed against me. What once was a cocoon was now a cage.

The room was a stark contrast to the living room with its white French Provincial sectional sofa and the grand pedestal lamp featuring the woman in Romanesque garb guiding her son and daughter through a storm. Decades of my mother's dreams and endless credit card payments had created that room as well as the adjacent dining room with its cherry wood furnishings and elaborate crystal chandelier.

The kitchen, on the other hand – with its pea green wooden cabinets and a table covered with a floral-print plastic tablecloth – told a different story.

Never renovated save for fresh coats of paint, it spoke of a family with modest beginnings and everyday struggles. This evening, as always, the second hand on the wall clock above the stove ticked loudly and relentlessly. To my mind, each tick marked more than one second. The never-ending ticks seemed to grow louder as they called to mind images of joy and fear.

In that room, I had seen the family's happy jumps and shouts when Darryl was accepted at the prestigious University of Detroit High School

I'd cringed here as the cries and insults of my parents' worst arguments replayed in my thoughts.

It was in this room that I'd felt shock, fear and anger after the assassination of Dr. Martin Luther King, Jr.

My family huddled together here during the heat and hate of Detroit's 1967 rebellion.

Ironically, I sat where every weekday before leaving for junior high and high school, I'd carefully arranged a cup of hot tea and a few cookies for Mom to enjoy when she returned home from nursing on the night shift. The notes I left were the most important part of the place setting. They usually included a little family joke, or a promise to follow my mom's advice to "put the icing on the cake" in an upcoming dance recital. The notes always said "'You're the very best mom in the whole universe – love you, love you, love you!"

Those notes had echoed what Mom gave me every day as I was growing up. Those big daily hugs before elementary school and the passionate words of confidence and encouragement would seep through my tender childhood skin and become embedded in my blood.

"Okay my little doll-face baby – you're the smartest and most beautiful little girl in the world. Mommy loves you so much – go get 'em and have a wonderful day!"

My mom was always at my side, it seemed, modeling class and style or explaining clearly the history behind the national and world news that fascinated me.

Then there was her determined savoir-faire – even when it was a bit over-the-top -- to protect me.

After my freshman year at Michigan State, during which I'd already secured a job at the campus newspaper, I applied for a summer internship with *The Michigan Chronicle*, the city's Black weekly newspaper. The interview with the editor, a bearded, officious and gruff older man, one Longworth Quinn, went badly and I wasn't hired

When I returned home in tears, Mom went into action. She grabbed the phone on the kitchen wall and immediately called the startled old editor. She laid into the man and laid him low.

"Mr. Quinn," she said, angrily. "You just treated my daughter very badly in an interview. I promise you – you will rue the day you treated her the way you did!"

Amazed at my mom's fierce lecture, I wiped my tears away and couldn't repress a laugh at her threatening "rue the day" phrase.

All the funny, frightening and tender moments of my family's turbulent years together surrounded me. My mom's fear that I was turning away from her was far from the truth.

It was just that I could not totally forget or abandon the father who, unfair as it was, had always treated me so well.

When I became the editor-in-chief of my suburban high school newspaper, a position that required that I often had to stay late after school to produce the school paper, he would drive the 20 miles to pick me up those evenings, even though he'd already worked a very long day.

"And you know," he would continue on many other occasions, "things at home," he would hesitate – "it wasn't all my fault. Your mother she made me do things, she, she . . . "

My reply was always as strong and firm as I could make it, to send a still respectful message that I'd accept no excuses for his treatment of Mom.

"Dad, I was there. I was there."

I let him know he'd lose any hope of a relationship with me if he ever spoke against my mom. It was an invisible line Dad realized he could not cross. And he never did.

That evening, I was anchored to the past, yet without a vision for my future. I longed for the chance to again follow my brother's lead, as I had so many times before.

Now Darryl faced his own dilemma as he tried to get through law school and a rocky marriage to his college girlfriend.

Indeed, marriage or grad school seemed to be the preferred escape route for most recent graduates to avoid returning to their childhood homes.

Fortunately, my parents had never pressed me to marry early. I hoped to have a family one day but decided that, given my parents' experience, marriage wasn't worth the risk in the near term.

As a few streaks of moonlight invaded the clear, frozen night outside the kitchen windows, I took hold of a simple and obvious solution: I'd apply to grad school, preferably out-of-state. It would be an adventure for me and prove acceptable to my mom who had always valued education as the best pathway to success. First, I'd repair any damage I'd done to the most important person in my life and then always maintain our deep connection.

When I finally packed my bags to leave, they were filled with lessons -- precious, bejeweled objects no one else could see - that would not be unpacked and examined for many years to come.

Conclusion:

Still I Rise

The emptiness in my childhood home was sadly unfamiliar two years after my parents' divorce. My mom lived alone in the house now and although her tears had ceased, it seemed to me they still flowed behind her cheeks. She was pleased and excited about my work at the Columbia University Graduate School of Journalism in New York City and felt comfortable about my choice to live in a dormitory on the campus.

And yet, when I came home to visit one weekend, the atmosphere was muted and I could tell my mom was still lonely.

A late-afternoon sunbeam that slanted just so across the living room and onto my cherrywood piano reminded me of after school piano practice. I longed for the smell of my favorite dinner – cornbread and vegetable beef stew – and the laughter of teenaged friends being teased by my mother. When I opened the door leading to the attic, ghosts invited me up the stairs to examine old keepsakes like the heavy black phone from my grandparents' home and my First Communion dress made of fine Polish lace that Mom had purchased so proudly.

I knew the old items and memories haunted my mother even more, suggesting that all her effort, each bit of love and hope for her family, had merely led to a vacuum. She said she felt she was living in a museum of our family's life, where she was the only one left to contemplate the paintings, to relive what was and imagine what might have been.

My parents' divorce proceedings had been wrenching as they fought over whether she would receive part of his government pension and whether they would eventually sell our home and divide the proceeds. In the end, a judge decided that she should keep the family home if she agreed to forego her right to part of his pension. So, Mom continued to work to maintain the home while Dad moved back to their first home that they still owned. Dad eventually bought another home. His adjustment would prove to be easier because he had the support of two brothers and two sisters in the city, who rallied to his side after the breakup despite the fact they knew my mom well.

But for now, my mother was alone and lonely, trying to build a new life as a single, older woman.

She continued her college courses at the University of Detroit Mercy, retreating deeply into books. I began to see that her retreat was her reward. She healed herself as she became immersed in poetry, philosophy and history. When I was home for a visit or during our regular long-distance talks, it was clear that my mother had taken in more than I had from several books I'd only read quickly in college.

She would quote *"The Prophet," by Kahlil Gibran:*

"Your children are not your children. . .

"You are the bows from which your children as living arrows are sent forth"

Another of her favorite books was *Viktor Frankl's "Man's Search for Meaning".*

Eventually, my mother became happier and more at peace with herself and the world through studying and reading other books that went well beyond her college texts. Later in life, she would beg me to never get rid of her great collection of books.

Mom found new energy and purpose in those years alone.

One day after checking her make-up and pinning on her nurse's cap in the first-floor powder room before leaving for work, mom said she saw an image that surprised her. Her face, though serious and lined, still looked younger than her 55 years. She left the house with a mustard seed of hope.

In addition to reading and studying, mom busied herself in those first years on her own by campaigning for city politicians she believed were honest and on the side of working people. She also began to enjoy her younger neighbors and their children.

Mom kept a ready stock of cold pop, potato chips and cookies for the kids on her block, who enjoyed seeking refuge on her front porch on long summer days or after school. They seemed to welcome her gentle teasing, her old sayings and even the grandmotherly advice she gave them along with the snacks.

My mom said she met Robert "Bob" Richardson, the definition of a tall, dark and handsome older gentleman at a block club meeting. He wasn't a neighbor but had been invited to stay for the meeting and dinner after doing some handyman work for his elderly aunt. After chatting, he asked if she'd be willing to continue talking by phone or go out for coffee, and she agreed.

My mother had already been noticed by several other men, so Bob's approach wasn't a surprise. Apparently, her nursing skills and financial independence – along with her good looks – made her something of a hot prospect. In most cases, my mother said she wasn't at all interested.

When I met Bob, I noticed his somewhat muscular build, sophisticated stance and sly sense of humor. He was full of the quick comebacks and the wise old country sayings Mom loved. Originally from Arkansas, he'd spent most of his career as a skilled technician for Ford Motor Co.

Bob had raised three children to adulthood, though his wife had died before he met Mom. He'd retired from Ford after 25 years. He enjoyed working to upgrade the two homes he owned and getting together with old friends to play cards and host cookouts. He was regularly introduced to middle-aged women who hoped they'd be 'chosen' by the attractive gentleman. Bob found the process tiring and saw no reason to give up his bachelor status for all the complications marriage could bring.

Mom said she saw in him a softness and an intelligence that she found attractive.

After a phone conversation and going to dinner, Mom decided to see if he would like to escort her to some of the shows and performances she really wanted to see.

"Who knows how long this will last," Mom told me, "So I might as well see if he likes the things I like."

Her new friend was indeed happy to take her to see the Ebony Fashion Fair Show. Then they took in a performance of the opera "Porgy & Bess" at Detroit's elegant Fisher Theatre.

I loved hearing that my mother was finally enjoying life.

Bob seemed thrilled with every one of my mother 's ideas and always showed up at her door dressed to the nines – his tie and pocket handkerchief always matched, complementing either a navy or gray suit. For each date, his midnight blue Mercury Grand Marquis – one of the top-of-the-line vehicles made by Ford – sparkled from a high gloss wax. After a few dates, he suggested one of his own – a romantic dinner at the restaurant on the top floor of the elegant Pontchartrain Hotel that sat near the banks of the Detroit River – called the "Top of the Pontch" - followed by a Lionel Richie and The Commodores concert.

Mom said the evening was more delightful than she'd imagined. When a small string and brass ensemble played at the restaurant before dinner, Bob insisted that she join him on the dance floor where he waltzed her around to the delight of the band and the other diners. Her suitor ended the dance with a bow before proudly escorting her back to their table.

Mom told me she loved Bob's attention and the wonderful courtship but added that trusting a man would not come easily for her after thirty-three years of a rough marriage.

Over the next year, Bob would propose to my mother at least three times. When she insisted that her home and any assets she had would be reserved for her children and could not be given to a husband, Bob was thrilled to let her know his substantial pension and savings would be more than adequate for their life together. He wanted nothing from her, he explained, but her hand in marriage.

"I had to marry her," he laughed when he later told his friends and my brother and me after they finally married, "to get her on my health insurance plan. At first, she refused to stop working even though I could offer her more than she was making working at the hospital. It was clear she needed mental health care!"

The couple settled into a comfortable, happy marriage – so comfortable that it allowed Mom to focus on my life once again.

Now that I'd completed my graduate degree from Columbia, Mom decided to visit me regularly in Baltimore, MD where I'd landed a job at *The Sun.* She seemed to think she could help me find an appropriate mate. It was her custom to arrive with the enticing aromas of a wonderful Southern dinner coming from her carry-on luggage – most often a Honey-baked Ham and a delicious cake or pie. I would invite friends over to enjoy the feasts.

Mom made lifelong friends and admirers among my new colleagues and friends. Mike Bowler, the *Sun's* leading education reporter with whom I worked closely, became a great friend of hers, as did his wife Margaret, who was from the Detroit area. First among equals, however, was a young man from Finland I dated for a while.

Antero Pietila, who was already established as a top reporter at *The Sun,* was more than happy to oblige when I asked him to show Mom around the city because I had to work one Saturday while she was visiting.

Antero planned a whirlwind tour of Baltimore, also known as Charm City. There was the harbor, where the Battle of Baltimore, fought during the War of 1812, was immortalized in the Star-Spangled Banner. The city's educated Black community had nurtured Frederick Douglass, who escaped enslavement and became a leading abolitionist. The late Supreme Court Justice Thurgood Marshall, who in 1954 had successfully argued the critical Brown school desegregation case before the high court, was also a Baltimore native.

And members of the city's old white ruling class – leaning, perhaps, on the renown of the poet Edgar Allen Poe and the scientific prestige of Johns Hopkins University - considered themselves the social and intellectual equals of the elite classes in Boston and New York City.

Mom was surprised that she was so warmly welcomed by this young man, whose bright personality and enthusiasm were perfectly matched by a headful of blond hair. This wasn't the suitor she expected, but because her daughter had trusted him enough to show her around Baltimore, and she'd had such a wonderful day, she certainly would not reveal the lesson she'd laid down for her daughter over the years.

She had always strictly instructed me that white men only wanted to use Black women for sex and were never to be taken seriously. She told me about the long, horrific history of white slaveowners using Black women for their own sexual pleasure and destroying Black families by selling children away from their parents and vice-versa.

Despite the apprehension she carried from a life begun in the old South and through the years as a Black woman working in a big city, Mom was fascinated by Antero. In a turnabout, she came to see what I had seen - that here was a fine man who saw America and its people clearly and yet regarded them with fascination and love. The young man eventually became her friend and an adopted son.

They were both bookworms, and he was especially interested in African American history and music. She loved the fact that he respected and agreed with her opinions on international issues as well as on American politics.

"Mrs. Richardson did you ever see Ella Fitzgerald in person. . . and what about that new documentary on the civil rights movement. . . and..."

It was the end of a long day and Antero looked toward the passenger seat of his car and saw he had talked his friend's mother to sleep.

Mom jolted awake as the car came to a stop in front of my apartment building.

"Oh my apologies for drifting off like that Antero. I've had a wonderful day. Thank you so much," she said as she headed into my building.

Long after Antero and I were no longer an item, Mom's friendship with him continued. He visited Mom and Bob in Detroit once while on a reporting trip there, and he kept in touch with them when he became a foreign correspondent, reporting from the Soviet Union and then South Africa.

He would be introduced over the years as" her son from Finland." Antero had lost his own mother early in life and he had suffered from a harsh relationship with his father who was a Lutheran pastor. Mom's warmth and affection seemed to fill empty spaces in his heart he had long ignored. She could see that he truly appreciated the loving attention her own children had taken for granted all their lives.

* * *

When I eventually married and, within a few years, produced two boys, Dana and Devon, Mom became a grandmother who was the human embodiment of a supernova in outer space – the powerful and luminous explosion of a massive star. Darryl's second marriage soon brought a third grandson, Evan, into her life.

Mom's energy was a major support to the toy industry – manifested in giant inflatable dinosaurs that appeared in her living room when the grandchildren visited one summer. At Christmastime, there was her always successful search for the most desired action figures of the 1990s – known as the Power Rangers.

Mom also developed a relationship with her beloved grandsons that could, like the colorful Northern lights or the fiery tail of a comet, surprise, and amaze anyone fortunate enough to see it.

I saw those cosmic lights clearly one night. My sons had just returned to Washington, DC after one of their two-week, end-of-summer visits with their grandma in Detroit.

Already in their pajamas, they'd gone outside to look at the beautiful, starry night sky with their dad, Warren Leary, a science journalist who wrote about space, technology and medical issues for The New York Times.

"Here's another firefly, Daddy! Can he fly all the way up to that Big Dipper?".

"No, son," my husband answered, laughing. "So far, people have flown to that great big moon you see there, but one day we might make it all the way to the stars."

Crickets were chirping and their late summer songs rode on a soft breeze that also picked up their wondrous childhood patter. The lovely sound drifted through the open front door and into the kitchen where I was clearing dinner dishes. The music made by the three loves of my life entered my heart never to be forgotten. I tucked the scene away in my memory to share with Mom in one of our frequent phone conversations. She would love to hear that story and many others – tales of precious moments like the ones from long ago I so clearly remembered with her at the center.

Later, as I tucked the boys into bed, their thoughts seemed as big as the night sky.

"Mommy, do you love Daddy more or do you love us more?" my eldest son, Dana, asked.

"Well," I began evenly. I'd learned to expect all manner of inquiry from them, especially at bedtime, when their sleepy little minds hung between two worlds.

"You know there are different kinds of love," I said. "For instance, it would be hard for your grandma to say whether she loved me more or she loved you guys more."

"No, it wouldn't," came the quick reply from the five-year-old child, now awake and sure he knew the truth.

"Grandma told us that she's done all she could do for you and Uncle Darryl and now she just loves us more," Dana said.

His middle name, Osborne, Mom's maiden name, was given to honor his grandmother and great grandfather. Mom was so enamored with her first grandchild; she called him her "Heart."

Devon, just two years younger than his brother, often continued talking as he fell asleep. Mom called her second grandson her "Brain," even though his toddler attempts at conversation tumbled from his mouth without a filter.

"Grandma is so great. She does so much for us, and we always have so much fun. You were really lucky to have her for a mommy.

"I . . . wish. . . I . . .had a mother like that," he said his voice dropping as his eyes fluttered to a close. "But Mommy you're. . . trying really. . .hard."

With those last words, both children were asleep, dreaming, no doubt, of their recent days with grandma.

Stunned, but somehow, not surprised, I kissed them both good night.

"Te amo mucho, mucho, mucho," I said, as I closed their bedroom door and whispered the final message I used every night. A small tear then crept down my cheek toward a smile.

Afterword

Our dinner was finished. Then tea and cookies, and a re-run of the old Sanford & Son show my mom so enjoyed. Spending weekends with her in her apartment, in a small, homelike building in Silver Spring, MD, was more precious than I would take the time to turn over in my hands. Now the memories are left to gently cradle in my heart.

I had oiled her scalp and brushed her hair, and then set the now straight, thinning gray locks on soft rollers. She was still so beautiful few would guess she'd seen 95 years.

I stayed with her overnight as often as I could because her memory failed her occasionally and with excruciating back pain often overtaking her, I worried about her wandering about the apartment, perhaps falling, and maybe even forgetting or regretting that she had moved to metropolitan Washington, D.C. to be near me.

To be near the daughter she would tell people she had raised like a "hot house rose." To be near her precious now grown-up grandsons, Dana and Devon, who took every opportunity to snuggle close to her once again, cell phones in hand.

"No Grandma, you punch in the number and push this button to talk, that one to hang up."

"Okay, my Heart; okay my Brain -- now show grandma again, I just forgot."

She'd started a new life in a strange place at eighty-five years old and made new friends – a band of angels from across the globe

- that seemed to see and understand everything that made my mom extraordinary.

Cherry Ipanag, her loving caregiver, was with her as much as I was, and surrounded her with the affection and energy of her entire Filipino family. Mom called her neighbors, Cynthia and Ulrich Cornelius, immigrants from Venezuela, her sister and brother. They were with her for coffee in the early mornings and for late night visits and personal care when neither Cherry nor I could be there.

When she finally moved to a family-run assisted living home, the proprietors, Maxine Francis and Paul Bama, of Jamaican and Cameroonian descent respectively, treated Mom as the honored queen of their household. Sue Hoover, a petite, energetic woman of English descent, helped by driving Mom to doctors' appointments, and Claire Morgan, a red-headed Irish woman, wrote kind little notes on the newspaper that she delivered to my mother each day. Antero, her "son from Finland" drove from Baltimore with his wife every week to visit his adopted mom. Darryl flew in from Michigan to see Mom frequently and loved her international support team, just as I did. There also was a virtual caravan of visitors – former neighbors, relatives from South Carolina, the grandchildren of her Saddler in-laws, and the many young people and their children she'd 'adopted' over the years.

She would say she was a tree too old to be moved. Perhaps, she was a tree with roots strong and deep enough to embrace all the true friends she met.

So, on this cold night in late fall, I brought with me the notes I'd made to summarize our many conversations, most of them taking place since her move to the area in late 2005.

There were her roots in the old South – a six-year-old share-cropper's daughter who screamed back at the white kids taunting her and telling them that she'd "rather be a niggah than po' white trash."

She came of age in Detroit, Michigan – living for a time with a doctor and his wife, adopting the hopes, dreams, and expectations of a wealthier class.

Then there was her love and strength through the harrowing years of her first marriage, her career as a nurse, working multiple jobs to afford her children's private schools and lessons, her love of literature, politics and her constant support of family and friends. She had lost Bob just eleven years after they married. My dad and almost all his extended family and hers had also passed away.

"Oh, baby," she said, her voice breaking with sadness and surprise, "You really remember all that – you really listened to me? You understood. . ."

There was the warm embrace; the few tears that ended the long disagreement between mother and daughter about this story we had both agreed I should write. The issue: she saw her life as a great tragedy; a story of accomplishments that could have been, ambitions crushed by circumstance and her own loyalty. I argued, half-blindly, that her life was a wonderful triumph.

Her story is like those of so many of the Black men and women of her generation who migrated from the old South to make what they could of life in cities like Detroit. The blossoming of the great character, values, and class that infused her soul became her great gift to her children, grandchildren and indeed, everyone she met.

I tell her story to honor her and the triumph given to me through her devotion.

Acknowledgments

Like so many others, I owe a debt of gratitude to the special gifts of Marita Golden, the award-winning author and professor of creative writing. Her ability to understand the story I'd held close to my heart for many years and to help me bring it to life was invaluable.

My dear friends and members of my writing group, the Sister Scribes, who advised and wept with me, chapter by chapter, also will never be forgotten.

I am grateful for the encouragement of my brother Darryl, the only person who knows the depth of the stories told and untold in this work. I also thank my adopted brother Antero Pietila for his wonderful help and listening ear as I put together the story of one of his dearest friends.

About the Author

Jeanne Estelle Saddler is a former journalist and communications director based in Washington, D.C. Her distinguished career included roles as a correspondent for *Time Magazine* and *The Wall Street Journal*, Counselor to the Administrator at the U.S. Small Business Administration, and Communications Director at the Metropolitan Washington Council of Governments. She now focuses on creative and powerful storytelling. *The Great Triumph – A Memoir of Courage and Devotion* is Saddler's first book.

www.ingramcontent.com/pod-product-compliance
Lightning Source LLC
Chambersburg PA
CBHW030305130626
46549CB00002B/702